I have had the humble pleasure c
of our wonderful church, and h̶a̶v̶e̶ ̶p̶o̶u̶r̶e̶d̶ ̶o̶v̶e̶r̶ ̶t̶h̶e̶ ̶c̶o̶n̶t̶e̶n̶t̶s̶ ̶o̶f̶ ̶t̶h̶i̶s̶
book. "His Name is Michael" grabbed my heart as I read through it,
and I could see the prompting of God to tell it like it is—no nonsense
truth, but totally invested in love.

Vikki Southwell has produced a work that is brave, vulnerable,
revealing, informing, full of grace, and can be a catalyst for healing
and restoration. Every child ever aborted is now living with their Maker
and has been redeemed by the Lord Jesus Christ. This is their eternal
reward. "His Name is Michael" is an amazing true story, crafted by the
Holy Spirit, as God provides forgiveness and healing. I commend this
work to all who dare to read it.

—**Rev Gary Brown**
Senior Pastor, The Vine Church, Yass, NSW

This is a courageous redemption story that will bring hope, strength
and self-worth to many women (and men), whether they are a teenager
or young mum, or a woman in her later years carrying the weight of
shame, guilt and unspoken trauma due to a regretful or misinformed
choice to abort their baby.

Vikki speaks as a woman who has journeyed from a place of brokenness,
through healing and into a genuine faith. She provides practical, doable
strategies undergirded by the encouragement needed to move forward
and expunge shame, resist lies, abandon fear and realise the power of
forgiveness. The reader is left knowing they are loved, beautiful and
equipped to live unashamed—through Jesus.

—**Ps Deb White**
Pastor, C3 Church Australia

What a powerful and poignant account of the realities and complexities surrounding teenage abortion! Vikki Southwell brings boldness and grace to an often-sidelined subject, offering readers a chance to process their own experience with understanding and hope. A highly recommended resource for those who work in the healthcare sector, pastoral care and church leadership—and for anyone whose life has been impacted by abortion.

—Anya McKee
Author of *Foreigners in the City of Silk,*
Feels Like I'm Breathing and *The Theatre*

Vikki Southwell writes with a raw honesty that will leave you in tears as she takes you on her journey through healing from the trauma of abortion. His name *is* Michael, and her beautiful mumma heart is fiercely determined to tell his story along with hers. In writing this book Vikki offers empathy and hope without judgement or condemnation. She shares her hope in Jesus Christ as her ultimate healer whilst acknowledging the value and importance of professional counselling and emotional support. Whether you have been through abortion or not, Vikki's story will resonate with you and give you greater understanding of trauma and hope for recovery. A beautifully woven and wonderfully written must-read.

—Katrina Wilkie
Author of *The 'B' Word*

Congratulations, Vikki on writing a truthful account of the pain and reality of abortion. I particularly love that this book gives practical ways of moving forward with God's help. I highly recommend this book to anyone who has undergone an abortion and wants to receive healing and restoration.

—Diane Watson
Abortion Healing Advocate

HIS NAME IS
MICHAEL

TORN CURTAIN PUBLISHING
Wellington, New Zealand
www.torncurtainpublishing.com

ISBN Softcover 978-0-6457827-9-0
ISBN EPub 978-0-6459696-0-3

Unless otherwise noted, all scripture is taken from the New International Version®, NIV®. Copyright © 1973, 1978, 1984, 2011 by Biblica, Inc.™ Used by permission of Zondervan. All rights reserved worldwide.

Scripture quotations marked NLT are taken from the Holy Bible, New Living Translation, copyright © 1996, 2004, 2015 by Tyndale House Foundation. Used by permission of Tyndale House Publishers, Inc., Carol Stream, Illinois 60188. All rights reserved.

Scripture quotations marked ESV are from The Holy Bible, English Standard Version®, copyright © 2001 by Crossway, a publishing ministry of Good News Publishers. Used by permission. All rights reserved.

Scripture quotations marked NKJV are taken from the New King James Version. Copyright © 1982 by Thomas Nelson, Inc. Used by permission. All rights reserved.

All details included in this book are written from the author's best recollection and perspective. Names of people included in this book are used with permission. Some names and identifying details of people described in this book have been altered to protect their privacy. This book is not intended as a substitute for professional counselling or medical advice.

Cover image by @eclipse_images. Licensed for commercial use: istockphoto.com

Typeset in Meta Pro, Meta Serif Pro and Quicksand.

Cataloguing in Publishing Data
  Title: His Name is Michael: Finding Hope in the Heartache of Teenage Abortion
  Author: Vikki Southwell
  Subjects: Christian Living, Biography, Abortion, Post-abortion Healing, Teenage
  Abortion, Abortion Recovery, Pastoral Care

A copy of this title is held at the National Library of Australia.

HIS NAME IS
MICHAEL

Finding Hope in the Heartache
of Teenage Abortion

Vikki Southwell

"Let the redeemed of the Lord tell their story."

Psalm 107:2

For the two tiny lives who are the bookends of this story . . . the beginning and the end, two lives so profoundly different yet so inextricably linked. This story could not have been written without either of you.

"For the Lord is good; his steadfast love endures forever, and his faithfulness to all generations."

Psalm 100:5 ESV

Contents

Introduction: This is Me

It was the weekend of my fortieth birthday and I was at a women's conference in Sydney, Australia. Following a brilliant message from Christian author and ministry leader Lisa Bevere about her recovery from anorexia nervosa, women were invited to come forward to the altar to receive healing from eating disorders. There were so many women trying to get to the front of the auditorium I was unable to return to my seat after ducking out to the bathroom. So, I sat on the stairs and soaked in the moment with my head in my hands. As I witnessed hundreds going forward for prayer, I felt the Holy Spirit speak to me, *"That will be you one day."* At that moment, I was given a clear picture of myself ministering to women, bringing the healing and hope of Jesus to victims of abuse and abortion.

Almost sixteen years later, I have had many opportunities to realise this vision, and many, if not more, setbacks along the way. In places where the subject of abortion is discussed with compassion and grace, I have been embraced and welcomed to share my story with a view to encouraging women and men to find healing, too. Yet there were also times when I was forbidden to speak because people thought it might "bring shame on the church's reputation." The stinging pain and humiliation these words caused me was like a slap in the face. In fact, a slap in the face would probably have hurt less. Unfortunately, this is a common attitude toward abortion, and I am more than likely not alone in this experience.

Even though I know I have been fully restored and redeemed in the eyes of Jesus, my story is still often viewed as a source of shame which must be kept hidden. How many of us have been told to be quiet because of someone else's insecurities? Even though I have often become discouraged and wondered if I should continue to persevere with this calling, I know that I can't give up; I won't give up. I believe this message is too important and needs to be delivered.

～

My experience is real, it is raw, and parts of it are very graphic and come with a trigger warning for those reading it. But, as it winds its way from beginning to end, it is also a message of incredible hope. While the focus of my story is primarily on abortion and its consequences, there are other experiences woven throughout my life that have shaped who I am. These include domestic violence, sexual abuse, pornography, adultery, divorce, and being let down by members of the church. While these are topics that people don't usually care to discuss, we need to keep talking about them. They are real issues affecting people every day, and they are too important to ignore.

It is my firm belief that in order to embrace true healing and move forward into the future, we must first acknowledge and deal with the painful events of our past. In sharing these details, particularly about the abortion process, I am not trying to be deliberately sensationalist, but I refuse to sugar-coat anything either. Real life is sometimes messy, and the messy should not have to stay hidden.

While I am truly sorry if my honesty causes anyone discomfort, authenticity is important to me. I gave up a long time ago trying to be something I'm not just to please others and fit in. I wasted many years of my life hiding my secrets and 'playing the part' so I would be accepted, wanted, and loved. Sadly, I learned along the way that sometimes you never fit in no matter how hard you try. Yet I have also discovered the wonderful truth that you don't always have to conform. Authenticity brings freedom and helps you find your 'tribe'—the people who offer you love and acceptance simply for being you. Maintaining a non-authentic version of yourself is exhausting because you must constantly remember who you're 'supposed' to be at any given time. Being genuine takes less effort and is so much more fulfilling!

∼

When I first started to write this book, I was hesitant about the reaction I would get. I struggled with the question, *What will people think of me?* I was quickly and gently reminded by the Holy Spirit that this was not about me. It was never about me. It is about Jesus and the redemption and forgiveness offered to us all through His death on the cross. I believe in the holy Trinity—Father, Son, and Holy Spirit—and my life is a testimony to the goodness of God. My story is written from a faith-based perspective, but whether you share my faith or not, I believe that somewhere in the pages of this book you will find truth and encouragement you can apply to the challenges you face in your life, too.

I am convinced we are meant to share our stories in order to encourage others that they are not alone. We've all experienced heartache because of poor choices, though everyone deals with their pain differently and some hurts are easier to resolve than others. I am sharing my story to show you that there can be light at the end of the tunnel, even when life takes you through some dark moments. Also, as someone who has experienced abortion first-hand, I feel a responsibility to share the truth about my experience in the hope it will discourage people from making similar choices and ultimately bring healing and closure to those who already have.

My story is not pretty and it's not perfect, but I make no apologies for that. This is me, and I am honoured and privileged to have you along for the ride. Let's do this!

CHAPTER ONE

Loss of Innocence

Childhood is a time of innocence, awe, and wonder. At least it should be. If I were to summarise my childhood in a word, it would be 'survival'. Much of my carefree innocence was stolen from me through the actions of others. Unless you have experienced it for yourself, it can be difficult to fully understand the enormity of the consequences of a tainted childhood—many of which are lifelong.

～

As was the cultural norm in those days, I have vivid recollections of alcohol-fuelled brawls between my parents. The adults of my generation worked hard and played hard, they loved hard, and they fought hard. There were many evenings where the after-dinner lull in our cul-de-sac would be interrupted by a screaming match from one of the neighbours' houses. I would seek refuge from these outbursts in the relative safety of my bedroom, huddled under the covers with my dog cowering next to me. My dad was very hot tempered, and it never took much to set him off. It was like living with Dr. Jekyll and Mr. Hyde—I never knew which one I would encounter at any given time—so much of my childhood was spent walking on eggshells. I did not often bring friends home for fear of what we might walk in to. Growing up, my dad was often distant toward me, and we didn't have a close relationship. He had grown up with only uncles and brothers, and before me had only sons. Since I was the first girl born into our family for many generations, I honestly don't think he knew what to do with me.

Sometimes, when they weren't fighting with each other, my parents would go out and leave me with a babysitter. On some occasions under the 'care' of my babysitter, I was sexually abused. I remember feeling so disgusted by what was happening to me, but as is typical with abusive situations, there was an imbalance of power. I felt like I had no choice.

When I summoned the courage to tell my mum, it ended up being a very difficult (and *very* awkward) conversation. I'm not sure what I was expecting by telling her, I just knew that I needed to tell her. And now, with the benefit of maturity, hindsight and empathy, I think she was probably stunned by my confession and just as grieved and confused as I was. She had trusted someone to look after me, and he had let us both down. I suspect she genuinely had no idea how to respond to my disclosure. Everyday sexual activity was never discussed in our family let alone sexual abuse. Still, that clumsy conversation with my mum did nothing to alleviate my confusion. In fact, if anything, it made it worse.

My childhood innocence was shattered, and my cry for help had gone unheeded. I was now a very impressionable and confused young girl who had more experience with certain intimate sexual acts than many adults, and I had not even reached puberty yet. I subsequently found myself on a journey of sexual dysfunction and unhealthy choices that would continue well into adulthood. The line between love and lust quickly became blurred, and I haphazardly tried to navigate the difference between the two. I longed for love but found only lust—mostly because I was looking in all the wrong places. *How was I supposed to find true love if I didn't even know what it looked like?* It wasn't until I had a monumental encounter in my late thirties with the living God, and discovered His love, that I began to realise my true worth.

~

I vividly remember how it felt to return to my childhood home as an adult. It had been many years since my family had moved out, and it was being sold by the current owners. When I saw there was an open house, my curiosity got the better of me, and I went back to take a look. Even though it had been beautifully renovated inside and out and looked like it deserved to grace the pages of a glossy magazine, the painful memories remained. The moment I walked into my old bedroom, besides thinking it was so much smaller than I remembered, the trauma of everything I had experienced came flooding back.

There is a scene in the movie *Forrest Gump* where Forrest and his friend Jenny return to her now-abandoned childhood home. As she stands outside the place where she had experienced abuse at the hands of her father, she begins to pick up stones and throw them at the house, starting slowly then using increasing force. Finally, she collapses onto the ground, exhausted and in tears. This is the painful reality for anyone who has experienced such trauma. It never truly leaves you.

CHAPTER TWO

Healing from Sexual Abuse

Sexual abuse against children is a heinous crime against one of society's most vulnerable groups of people. If you are a survivor of sexual abuse, let me start by saying how sorry I am that this happened to you. It is tragic to think there are so many others like me who have had their childhoods stolen. In my experience, healing from sexual abuse can be a lifelong process, especially if it is not acknowledged and dealt with effectively.

One of my favourite quotes summarises it like this: "If you don't heal from what hurt you, you will bleed on people who didn't cut you." Simply put, if you don't receive the help you need, your open wounds will continue to impact you and your loved ones for the rest of your life. You will end up pushing people away, and innocent parties, including you, will end up paying the price for crimes they didn't commit.

While there is sadly no quick fix, I want to share some advice that I hope will help you heal and find freedom from childhood abuse in order to move forward with your life.

1. Acknowledge the Child Who Was Abused

In many cases, the voice of the child who was abused does not come out until they have reached adulthood and can finally and fully articulate what happened to them. It's important, therefore, to give your inner child a voice and allow them to be heard. I used to think a lot about what I would say to my younger self from the perspective of my grown-up self. I would tell her I'm sorry she wasn't listened to and that what happened to her was swept under the rug. I would tell her it wasn't her fault, and that her identity is not tied to that experience. I would tell her she turns out okay despite what was done to her, and she mustn't let it affect her grown-up relationships. But mostly, I think I would just want to wrap her in my arms and give her a big hug.

2. Find Your Identity in Who You Are, Not What Was Done to You

It took me forty years to figure this out. Your identity is not rooted in how you were treated by others. In fact, the way others treat you says significantly more about them than it does about you. The sooner you understand this, the better the rest of your life will be. No one on earth will love you unconditionally and without reserve. But Jesus does. He loves you so much that He died for you, and He died so you could live in abundance. As He says in John 10:10: "The thief comes only to steal and kill and destroy; I have come that they may have life, and have it to the full."

3. Talk About It

It is not healthy to bury trauma in the hope it will go away, because it never will until you face it. You can only keep something buried for so long until it eventually comes back to bite you anyway, one way or another. The longer you leave it, the messier it's going to be when it does finally come to the surface.

I recommend seeing a counsellor if you need to. Receiving counselling is not indicative of weakness; it is a sign of a strong person admitting they need help. A close confidante can also be helpful, but as a word of caution, be careful to whom you choose to divulge your personal experiences. You don't want to become the subject of gossip. A confidante should be a trustworthy person who has perhaps even walked this journey successfully already. If your confidante is as broken as you are, your time together may become a mutual pity party, feeding each other's pain and causing more harm than good.

As an adult, I had the opportunity to talk to my abuser about what had happened to me as a child. He showed remorse, and while I don't think I will ever fully understand why he behaved in the way he did, our conversation provided a degree of healing and restoration for me that would not have been possible otherwise. While this was my experience, I recognise it is not feasible for everyone. It may not be practical or safe to have that conversation, and that is perfectly okay. You should never under any circumstances put yourself in an uncomfortable or unsafe situation. Toxic people from your past do not deserve a place in your present if they have not changed or accepted responsibility for their actions, and even if they have, it is still your prerogative to decide whether to let them back in.

You have the right to set whatever boundaries you need to in your healing journey, and no one else is entitled to take you on a guilt trip just because they don't like or agree with them.

4. Choose to Forgive

Forgiving your abuser is one of the hardest things you will ever have to do. It is also an action that will bring you significant healing.

Forgiving a toxic person from your past is different from allowing them a continued role in your present. It is entirely acceptable to forgive someone while keeping them at arm's length. In some circumstances, this is not only wise but safe. Your healing cannot be complete while you are still unhealthily engaging with the person who hurt you. The Bible commands us to forgive (see Matthew 6:12; Mark 11:26), but we are under no obligation to allow them to remain in our lives. Forgiveness sets us free to make that choice.

Forgiving yourself is non-negotiable if you want to heal from the wounds of your past. Acknowledging that the abuse you suffered was not your fault is an important but difficult step. It is natural to wonder if we did anything to deserve what happened to us. The answer is absolutely not! Children should never be blamed for being seductive or inviting sexual behaviour, and anyone attempting to use this absurd argument to justify the abuse of children does not deserve the mental energy it requires to try and convince them otherwise.

5. Be Honest With Yourself and Your Spouse

Your sexuality is a God-given gift which can and should be a beautiful thing. Yet even as a grown woman, I still struggle with the sexual advances of my husband at times. It can be difficult to have an honest conversation with your partner about your previous sexual trauma, but it is vital if you want to enjoy a fulfilling relationship. They are not the cause of your trauma, and it's important to talk openly with them, so it does not become a source of conflict in your relationship. Communicating with your spouse in this way requires a lot of grace and sensitivity from both sides, especially as emotional triggers and memories unexpectedly resurface.

It is possible to learn the beauty of lovemaking but it does take time. Years and years of unresolved baggage will not just disappear overnight, but as you learn to let yourself relax and allow your spouse to love you the way God intended, you will discover that there is a whole new world of positive sexual experiences to explore and enjoy!

"Come, my beloved, let us go to the countryside, let us spend the night in the villages. Let us go early to the vineyards to see if the vines have budded, if their blossoms have opened, and if the pomegranates are in bloom—there I will give you my love. The mandrakes send out their fragrance, and at our door is every delicacy, both new and old, that I have stored up for you, my beloved."

Song of Songs 7:11-13

CHAPTER THREE

You're What?

The year was 1984. I was sixteen years old and had miraculously managed to finish high school the previous year. It had not been a particularly happy time in my life, and I wasn't disappointed to see the end of it. I ended up moving to a different high school after two years because of painful bullying. I'm not proud to admit that I too began to bully those weaker than me and subsequently became a classic example of the saying, 'Hurting people hurt people'.

I was one of those kids whose report cards always said, "Could have tried harder." I believed I was dumb, so I hardly ever finished or handed in assignments. For an entire term of music class, I hid my flute in my locker so I wouldn't have to participate in any performances. I'm sure the teacher knew I was lying when I told her I'd lost it, but perhaps she figured that since I didn't care, she didn't have to either. Although the last two years of high school were slightly better than the first, my teachers were likely just as relieved to see the back of me as I was of them. I only had one close friend, until she hooked up with the boy she knew I liked during our final school holidays. This only reinforced my belief that not only was I dumb, but I was also unlovable and no one deserved my loyalty.

After scraping through my high school years by the skin of my teeth, any future career dreams I once had quickly disappeared. I had always wanted to go into the field of psychology and counselling—I guess even back then I had a natural tendency to want to help people, particularly those in underprivileged and remote communities. However, I let my fear of others stop me from immediately pursuing that dream. Ultimately, I chose not to go to college because I was too afraid to face my high school bullies who had gone before me. Although I did go on to study counselling later in life, at that point in time I was left with literally no idea what I was going to do next.

~

Most of my young life had been spent wanting to be invisible to avoid drawing attention to myself, yet at the same time I was secretly and desperately craving that same attention. As a shy, awkward and fast-developing young teenager, I thought any attention was better than no attention at all, which led me into many situations that, in hindsight, I should have avoided at all costs. I always ended up in the 'wrong crowd' but was only ever a fringe-dweller, never fully accepted.

It pains me to admit that in my foolish desire to be included and popular, I succumbed to peer pressure and made unwise choices including smoking, underage drinking, soft-drug experimenting, wagging school, and pitifully trying to get boys to notice me—which they never did. In the process, I earned some very unappealing nicknames. My reputation was not something I was proud of, and it was made worse by the fact that much of it was untrue and unwarranted. The people spreading rumours based their opinions on my outward actions and had no idea of the 'real' me desperately crying out to be seen.

As I reflect on those days, it saddens me to realise the 'friends' I fell in with weren't really my friends. I was simply their puppet, and they held me tightly by the strings. Truthfully, they were probably just as insecure as I was. They just masked it better.

When a girl I knew from school invited me to a bush dance (yes, it was the 1980's!) with members of her church youth group, it was with more than a little hesitation that I said yes. I didn't know at the time that saying yes to that invitation would change the course of my entire life. Back then, trust did not come easily to me, and I allowed very few people access into my world. I had spent many years carefully constructing walls around my heart to protect myself from getting hurt and seldom let my guard down. Once bitten, twice shy, my past experiences had made me wary of others. Expecting the worst, it felt safer to keep people at arm's length rather than expose myself to the pain I knew would inevitably come. So, when I met Jack at my friend's bush dance and he liked me for who I was, my sixteen-year-old heart fell fast and hard.

From the moment he asked if he could drive me home from the dance, I truly believed he was 'the one'. He was from a good Christian home, and he seemed different from all the other boys. He told me his father was a local business owner and they appeared to be well respected in the community and in their church. Jack seemed like the perfect package, and I allowed my heart to dream about our future together. Besides, we met at a Christian youth dance. What could possibly go wrong?

At eighteen, Jack was two years older than me and had his own car—a 'Ute' with a bench seat which was perfect for snuggling up close to him as he drove. We quickly became inseparable, spending every spare minute together. Within weeks, our relationship had progressed to being boyfriend and girlfriend. I was lovestruck and thought I was so grown up in my first real relationship. I had our future all planned out from our wedding right down to the house on the farm with the white picket fence enclosing the yard where our children would one day play. All the hurt and pain from my childhood paled in comparison as I blossomed in the wonder of finally being 'loved'.

Jack was my escape from the volatility of my family home. I looked forward to the sound of his car as he drove into my driveway to whisk me away from my difficult reality for a short time. We would spend hours driving to secluded spots, usually ending up half-naked as we explored each other's bodies and our awakening sexuality. On one such trip, I freely gave him my virginity.

We were young, starry-eyed, and clearly not clever enough to register that unprotected sex would eventually lead to an unplanned pregnancy. Call me naive, but the thought honestly never entered my mind. But just a few months after we began dating, during one of our secret nights of passion, our baby was conceived on the bench seat of his car.

~

"You're pregnant, aren't you?"

It was more a statement of fact than a question as my mum stood in the doorway of my bedroom after I had thrown up for the umpteenth time that day. I shrugged my shoulders and turned away, unable to look her in the eye or confirm her suspicions. Although I hadn't had it confirmed, I had missed my period and along with the accompanying nausea, I knew deep down her intuition was correct.

I could sense my mum's disappointment in the realisation that her youngest child and only daughter had so spectacularly let her down. But at the same time, I knew she loved me, and I was confident she would support me in raising the new life that was growing inside me. Still, that didn't make telling her any easier, and I was grateful that she opted to tell my dad instead of making me do it. To my relief, despite his own disappointment in what I had done, he didn't fly off the handle in a fit of rage as I was expecting but also supported me in this unexpected turn of events. I don't recall us ever considering any alternative option like having the baby adopted once it was born, and the idea of an abortion was never even mentioned. I'm not even sure I knew what an abortion was at that point, and even if I did, it would have been the furthest thought from my mind.

My parents were far from perfect, and my adolescence was rocky for all of us, but to their credit, they were very matter-of-fact about the whole thing. I don't believe it ever occurred to any of us that I would not continue with the pregnancy and give birth to this baby, and if the thought ever did occur to my parents, they never said. Jack's parents, on the other hand, were less supportive. His mother immediately called a meeting to discuss the predicament we had found ourselves in.

I vividly remember sitting in my parents' living room as Jack's mother told me in no uncertain terms that this baby would not be allowed to live. Despite my feeble protests, his mother was adamant. She was clearly the dominating force in their family, and her mind was made up. Protecting her family's reputation and saving her son from a scandal was clearly more important to her than protecting the life of my unborn child—*her* grandchild. Jack, sitting beside me, kept his mouth firmly shut. I didn't know whether he was scared of his mother or freaked out by the thought of becoming a father—perhaps a bit of both.

Whatever his reasons, he failed to stand up for me or our unborn baby, leaving me alone to try and fight for both of us. It was a fight I was never going to win. I felt coerced by Jack's parents into a decision I neither asked for, nor wanted. As far as they were concerned, the matter was settled. I would terminate my pregnancy and snuff out the life I should have been protecting and nurturing. The very thought of it repulsed every fibre in my being. Still, I was not strong enough or confident enough in my convictions to fight them. If I had been more educated in foetal development and abortion procedures, I'm sure I would have fought harder. But I was only sixteen years old. In many ways, I was still a child myself. I was flat out trying to decide what to do on the weekend, let alone making a life-changing decision like this one. I honestly had no idea how far-reaching the consequences would be.

I remember from that point onwards, everything happened very fast. I was already twelve weeks pregnant and there was an element of urgency to 'get it done'. I felt like I was having an out-of-body experience as plans were quickly put into place around me while I silently and obediently complied with everyone else's wishes and demands. It was though I had been sucked into a vortex with no idea how to escape.

My dreams of the farm and the white picket fence had turned into a living nightmare, and I just wanted to wake up and for it all to be over.

CHAPTER FOUR

The Truth No One Tells You

**This chapter comes with a trigger warning for graphic and
potentially upsetting content related to abortion.*

"Where is your mum?" It was a couple of weeks after my seventeenth
birthday and the night before our scheduled abortion appointment.
Jack's mother had driven him to my house where he would stay in our
spare room. The following morning we would leave very early with
my parents, as we had to drive interstate to have the procedure done.
In those days abortion was still illegal or inaccessible in many places,
so our options were limited.

I had heard the car pull up and was expecting to see them both, but
Jack had arrived at my door alone, prompting me to ask the question
about where his mother was. His reply took me by surprise: "She's in
the car." He told me she had declined to come in with him because
she was wearing her slippers and did not want to get them dirty by
getting out of the car.

Really? I thought. *I am just about to terminate the life of your grandchild
and you won't even face me because you are wearing your slippers!* In

that moment, it felt like my one job was to dispose of this 'problem', and she wanted nothing more to do with it. If only it was that simple.

I wonder now how my own parents must have felt as we drove in silence to the abortion clinic almost four hundred kilometres away. Lost in my own little world of grief and confusion, it saddens me to say I honestly never gave their feelings a second thought. *Were they hurting as much as I was? Were they feeling just as pressured into this decision as I was?* I'll never know. They didn't mention it, and I never asked. Maybe I couldn't bear to find out. Now that I am a parent myself, I can't even begin to comprehend what it must have been like for them. They lost a grandchild too—and they had a rebellious daughter who caused them shame and embarrassment, and certainly more pain than they deserved. Still, they chose to fully support me through the whole experience for which I am so grateful.

~

The waiting room of an abortion clinic is a strange, unfamiliar place. Heads were bowed low to avoid making eye contact, but the reality is, you don't need to look at someone to know how they might be feeling in a place like this. Since abortion was much less available and harder to access back then, it reinforced the sense of isolation and shame for those of us who made the difficult choice to have one.

It was a very different experience when I had my two children sometime later. An obstetrician's waiting room is usually full of excited chatter with expectant mums comparing notes about their baby's development. Meanwhile, an abortion clinic waiting room is a sombre place, everyone lost in their own thoughts and questions. *Are they here because they were coerced like I was, or did they make the choice themselves? Is it her first time, or has she done this before? What will it feel like? How will I feel after it is done?*

The answers to those last two questions I had to find out for myself. Nobody counselled me on what would happen or how it would feel. Nobody told me I would be able to see and hear everything that happened as my baby's tiny body was violently torn apart while his life was literally sucked out of me. Nobody told me how you could be in a room full of people and feel so utterly alone. Nobody told me about the guilt and shame I would carry for years until I could finally acknowledge and grieve what I had done. Nobody told me the consequences of this decision would be long and far reaching, plaguing me for the rest of my life.

Even now, when I look back, a gut-wrenching cry rises from the bottom of my heart: *WHY DIDN'T ANYBODY TELL ME?!*

~

I will never pass judgement on a woman who has had an abortion, although I will actively try to dissuade someone who is contemplating having one. *Why?* Because I know what it feels like. I know how it feels to carry guilt and be on the wrong end of condemnation. I know how it feels to have to hide your shameful secrets. But more than that, I know how it feels to lay in a cold, sterile room with no one even allowed in there to comfort me or hold my hand. I know how it feels to lay on a gurney with my feet up in stirrups, unable to turn away as the jar attached to the suctioning tool filled and turned red with the blood of my baby as it mixed with mine, to then be casually discarded by people who were just 'doing a job'. I know how it feels to never be able to erase that memory from my mind.

It may be a graphic description, but this is the cold hard truth. Choosing to have an abortion is a deeply personal and life-altering decision, usually made at a time of intense emotional turmoil. That is why women considering abortions need to be made aware of the consequences of their decision. As a gullible teenager, I had been deceived into believing that if my pregnancy was terminated before twelve weeks, no harm was done as 'it' was not yet fully formed. But Psalm 139:13-14 says:

> *"For you created my inmost being; you knit me*
> *together in my mother's womb. I praise you because*
> *I am fearfully and wonderfully made; your works are*
> *wonderful, I know that full well."*

And Jeremiah 1:5 reiterates:

> *"Before I formed you in the womb I knew you, before you*
> *were born, I set you apart . . ."*

My goal here is not to engage in a pro-life versus pro-choice argument, although I will happily discuss it with anyone who is open to having a reasonable and respectful conversation. We are all free to make our own choices, but there are always consequences to every choice we make. It's important, therefore, to do your research and make an informed decision instead of being fooled. The truth is, no matter how much you might try to gloss over it, if you have an abortion, you are killing another human being. I know I would have fought harder for my baby if I had truly understood that.

Here's what I know now that I didn't know then. At twelve weeks gestation my baby had a heartbeat, a brain, and ten fingers and toes. He was tiny but fully formed . . . and he had a soul. He was not just a bunch of cells waiting to turn into a baby at some magically appointed time as I had been led to believe (I struggle to believe the people trying to justify abortion still espouse this theory today!). My baby was a living being, he was loved, and his life was brutally cut short before it even began. He would never realise his God-given potential, he would never grow up, and I would never get to hold him in my arms.

CHAPTER FIVE

Healing from Abortion Trauma

Abortion is such an emotive topic, which is one of the reasons I am compelled to write this book. There are strong opinions on either side of this issue, and very little middle ground. Fanatics on both sides of the pro-choice versus pro-life argument sometimes do more harm than good for their cause, and I think the Church often sits somewhere in between. I've been in churches where it is almost forbidden to discuss such subjects let alone minister to the people involved, and I've been in others where abortion is not only discussed but dealt with in a compassionate and sensitive manner. The second option is far better.

In his blog, *Abortion is Everyone's Issue*, Pastor Matt Chandler writes: "As the church we must not say of abortion, 'This is murder,' without saying to pregnant women, 'We will serve you.' If we're doing the former without the latter, we aren't truly understanding the gospel."

I love that. If we can't support and love these women in our churches, we've missed the point of the gospel entirely. I guarantee you that on any given Sunday there are women sitting amongst us silently struggling with their abortion guilt—women who can't share their shameful burdens because others don't know how to deal with them, or worse, don't want to.

Perhaps it's because we've been led to believe that 'good Christian girls' don't do that kind of thing. Believe me, they do. Good Christian girls can get pregnant out of wedlock. So why isn't anyone trying to understand and comfort them? Why isn't anyone counselling them to make better choices? Instead, we just cast them aside because we don't know what else to do with them. When did we get so caught up in 'doing church' that we forgot how to 'be' the Church?

This attitude makes me angry. In my view, it is better to refrain from offering an opinion on something you will never understand. One of my favourite scripture verses is found in John 8:1-11 when the teachers of the law ask Jesus to pass judgement on a woman who was caught in the act of adultery. After they had left, Jesus asked her:

> *"'Woman, where are they? Has no one condemned you?' 'No one, sir,' she said. 'Then neither do I condemn you,' Jesus declared. 'Go now and leave your life of sin.'" (v. 10,11)*

This is profoundly beautiful in its simplicity. The woman received no condemnation but was instead set free to choose a better path.

It saddens me that there are critical and judgemental Christians in our world like the teachers of the law in this story who were trying to find justification to stone the woman to death. But Jesus' response to them is powerful. When they kept on questioning Him, Jesus straightened up and said to them, "Let any one of you who is without sin be the first to throw a stone at her" (v. 7). Likewise, none of us can fit into that category. We are all sinners in need of grace. Jesus actively sought out the misfits and the outcasts. He didn't judge them by what they'd done, He loved them for who they were. *Should we not be doing the same?*

Please hear me: I am not condoning abortion. Abortion is evil. But women who have had abortions are not evil. There are certainly those who have chosen to have abortions for frivolous reasons, but there are also many women and girls like me who feel like they had no choice but to make this impossible decision or were misinformed about the whole process. They need our compassion, support, and love, not our judgement and criticism. I will continue to fight for these women so that they too can experience healing and restoration and live a life free from shame.

While my target audience for this topic is obviously women, I also want to acknowledge the many men who also suffer from abortion trauma. These include men who have had their chance at fatherhood cruelly ripped from them by a woman who didn't want to be a mother. They may have desperately wanted to raise a child but were never given the chance because of the 'her body, her choice' mentality. Nobody usually thinks about these men, but they are out there, and their grief and pain are just as valid.

I'm not sure that abortion trauma is something you ever fully 'get over' but with the right support, I think it's something you can learn to live with. Here are some additional suggestions that have helped me on my own healing journey.

1. Acknowledge and Give Your Child a Name

For me, acknowledging that this was a real person instead of the clump of cells I had been deceived into thinking it was, was pivotal to my healing. It's easy to disregard an inanimate object and remain in denial about what happened, but you can no longer remain ambiguous when you personalise them. You have no choice but to face the facts and deal with the undeniable truth that you were responsible for ending your child's life. This revelation is painful to acknowledge and is incredibly distressing and confronting. Your healing will not happen overnight. This is a long process of grief, and it is a process that you have to go through, but it will eventually lead to acceptance and peace.

Please also consider seeking counselling from a qualified abortion grief counsellor. Often just taking the brave action of seeing a counsellor and acknowledging your abortion is a significant step in the healing process.

2. Forgive Yourself and Others

I cannot stress this enough: You will not be able to heal without forgiving yourself for the part you played in ending your child's life. A crucial part in forgiving yourself is to also seek forgiveness from God. This is a very difficult step as it involves admitting you have blood on your hands. I still cringe when I hear people use the word murder when talking about abortion. But Jesus died for the murderers among us—even those who didn't understand what they were doing. And He continues to intercede for us to receive God's forgiveness. Jesus said, "Father, forgive them, for they do not know what they are doing" (Luke 23:34). I found that acknowledging and naming my child and asking God to give me an image to hold on to helped me to think about him with hope and peace rather than regret and shame.

One of the hardest things I have experienced, however, is a lack of acknowledgement from the other people involved in my abortion decision. I may have forgiven them, but I have still not received the closure I would like. The unfortunate truth is that while this closure may never come, my decision to forgive them is not dependent on whether they are sorry, or indeed, whether they even acknowledge their role in what happened. This can be difficult to digest, and it takes a lot of inner strength to forgive someone despite how they may have behaved toward you. But if you do, you will ultimately find the freedom to move on from your guilt, shame, and grief.

3. Say Goodbye

It can be helpful to hold a special ceremony to recognise and honour your child, commemorate their loss, and lay your memories to rest. Saying goodbye in this way can also offer much-needed closure and give you an opportunity to grieve properly. You need to allow yourself to grieve. Let the tears come, and don't try to hold them back. I cannot emphasise this enough.

I used to feel guilty when I compared my experience to women who had suffered a miscarriage. It didn't feel appropriate for me to grieve my loss in the same way because I made a choice about ending my baby's life, and they didn't. I know this is a very sensitive point, and please understand I am in no way minimising the pain and sorrow of miscarriage. But the truth is, regardless of the circumstances, losing a baby is always a significant bereavement and must be recognised as such. Your baby's life mattered. Don't let anyone tell you otherwise.

4. Let Go of Your Shame

Along with sincere regret, my decision to have an abortion left me with a profound sense of shame. Shame doesn't just say you *did* something bad; shame says you *are* a bad person and bad people don't deserve mercy or compassion. Shame keeps you silent and isolates you even from those closest to you. Shame is a liar from the pit of hell.

A few weeks after I had my abortion, I was at Jack's house with the rest of his family. It would be the last time I ever interacted with any of them. In retrospect, I don't know what we were trying to achieve with this gathering. I was acutely aware of the uncomfortable atmosphere in their house, and if the ground had opened up and swallowed me then and there, I would have been very grateful. Yet I vividly remember Jack's dad coming over to talk to me. Putting his arm around my shoulders, he asked me how I was. It was the kindest thing anyone in Jack's family ever did for me. In an instant, he had done what no one else could or would do: He recognised my pain and acknowledged me as a person who had been through a horrific experience. Amid my shame, *he saw me*. It wasn't until many years later that I realised how significant that moment was. It is something I will never forget.

~

Finally, I would encourage you to read the book *Tilly* by Frank E. Peretti. This is a deeply moving story which beautifully captures the restoration, forgiveness, and hope that is possible for parents who have lost a child through abortion. Containing glorious imagery of aborted children growing up in Heaven, I thoroughly recommend it as a tool to help you move forward in your own journey of recovery and healing.

CHAPTER SIX

The Aftermath

Following the abortion, my heart was shattered. Despite what abortion advocates will tell you, it is not a simple procedure. It is horrific. It is barbaric. In fact, there are not enough adjectives to describe how awful it is. Yet, I was given no medical or emotional support to aid my recovery. Instead, I was sent away from the clinic with what felt like nothing more than a pat on the head and a packet of contraceptive pills. The job was done, and my baby and I had become little more than a statistic.

I should have allowed myself time to heal physically and emotionally, but I didn't. I don't think I have ever felt lonelier in my life. My dad never spoke of the abortion again, and it was only when I was a young married woman with children of my own that I was able to talk about it with my mum. It was then that I finally realised the extent of the pain it had caused her. She had grieved for me, her daughter, and for her unborn grandchild, yet she carried it alone—as I had.

∼

While I had conveniently absolved Jack and his family of the responsibility of an unwanted pregnancy and released them to go on with their lives as if nothing had happened, I was left holding hundreds of tiny broken pieces of my heart which I had neither the inclination nor the energy to even try to put back together. I was depleted, but more than that, I was bone dry. It felt like a part of me had died along with my baby that day, and in a sense, it had. It would be a long time before I would feel fully restored.

Jack thought we could continue in our relationship as though nothing had changed, including immediately resuming our sexual activity. But I couldn't go back to the way things were before. *How could I just dismiss everything I had been through and 'move on'?* Jack would never understand how traumatic this experience was for me, and I could certainly never look his mother in the eye again. The damage was too huge to overcome, and I broke up with him not long afterwards.

After ending our relationship, I became sexually involved almost straight away with another guy. I neglected to take the contraceptive pills the abortion clinic had given me, and within months I discovered I was pregnant again. Once again, my world was thrown into chaos, and I knew I was putting my parents through unbelievable disappointment and heartache. But I was determined to give this baby a chance, even if I had to do it on my own. Even though I didn't know how I would manage it, I was certain of one thing—I was never going back to that abortion clinic.

Despite thinking I was ready to grow up, the truth is I wasn't ready at all for that level of responsibility, and I made a lot of mistakes. There are many things I wish I had done differently. Carrying baggage from one experience into the next does not relieve you of that burden, it just creates more weight. To use a travel analogy, I should have checked some of my excess baggage at the gate before boarding the next flight! It took me a long time to learn that if I had dealt with my unresolved issues earlier, I could have avoided a lot of unnecessary heartache for myself and those I later became responsible for. I know many of my parenting decisions would have been different if I had taken the time to be healed from my insecurities.

At the tender age of seventeen, I was hastily married in a shotgun wedding. As a little girl, I used to dress up in my mum's wedding dress, imagining myself riding off on a white horse with my Prince Charming. I did wear her dress on my wedding day—altered to cater for my rapidly-growing pregnant belly—but I was not going to have the fairy-tale ending I had dreamed about. Not yet anyway. Sometimes the heroine of the story has to kiss a few frogs on her way to finding her knight in shining armour!

~

I was still a kid myself, and now I was five months pregnant. *What did I know about being married and having a baby?* It wasn't long before reality set in. My daughter was born two days after my eighteenth birthday, and my son just before I turned twenty. They were my miracle babies, and the first things in my life I could be truly proud of.

Being a new mum is hard at the best of times, but as a broken seventeen-year-old girl, I found out very quickly that running from your problems doesn't make them go away, they just follow you. Despite trying my best, I still got so many things wrong. I sometimes think back and wonder how I muddled through those early years. I am so grateful and very blessed that my kids turned out as well as they did, despite having a very flawed mum!

I had been married for three years with an almost three-year-old and a not-quite-one-year-old when my partner suddenly decided he'd made a mistake. Ironically, using the same excuse Jack has since used for the abortion, he declared he was not actually ready to be a father and he needed to 'find himself first'. *Hmm okay. It probably would have been good for you to have had this epiphany before now,* I thought, *but off you go. You go ahead and have a nice life, and I'll stay here and raise our children on my own.*

Once again, I was left to figure things out on my own. Interestingly, this development marked a drastic change in my relationship with my parents, especially my dad. He had mellowed a lot over the years, and had softened significantly since the birth of my children. I loved watching him interact with them; it was as though someone had literally turned on a light inside of him. Although it was never discussed, I think we both knew something had changed between us, and it was the best outcome I could have hoped for. When he died six years later from a massive heart attack, I was heartbroken. It was very sudden and there was no time to say goodbye, but I was with him when he died and the last words spoken between us before he collapsed were filled with love. For that I will be forever grateful.

My ex-in-laws were also wonderfully supportive during this time. Even after their son left, they remained very involved in the lives of their grandchildren (and mine, even after I re-married). My mother-in-law, who was an English teacher, would catch three buses from her house on the other side of town to ours so she could take the kids on their regular outing to the library. My daughter now takes her own children on bus rides, "just like we used to do with Grandma."

In a world where so many ex-partners wilfully estrange their children from their extended family, I made a deliberate choice that my ex-in-laws would not pay the price for their son's actions. They were not responsible for his decisions, so why should they be punished for them? I'm thankful that we continued to have a close relationship until they both passed away when my children were young adults.

CHAPTER SEVEN

Tarnished Trophy Wife

At the tender age of twenty, I was a divorced single mum. My relationship choices up to this point had been sensational failures. You might think I'd have learned from my mistakes, but you would be wrong. If anything, my pattern of unhealthy decision-making just continued to get worse.

About a year after my divorce, I became involved with a guy who was much older than I was. As a young, insecure and impressionable woman, I think I was good for his ego—someone he could brag about to his friends. He lied to me about his age when we first met which should have been my first red flag. There were many things that, in hindsight, I should have picked up on, but in my desperate need to be loved and cared for, I completely ignored the warning signs. With two young children to think about, instead of only me, how I wish I had been stronger and wiser!

My second marriage lasted almost twenty years, and though much of it was good, it was unhealthy on many levels. Our arguments—of which there were many—would often mirror those I had witnessed as a child, complete with shouting, flying fists, and smashing plates. No one had ever modelled for me how to handle conflict or confrontation well, so I defaulted to what I knew. I didn't know how to do it any differently. Like my mother before me, I became good at hiding my bruises and avoiding social engagements. My husband was also a product of his upbringing, raised in a culture where 'blokes were blokes' and women were to be seen and not heard—and readily available whenever their partner wanted something. This was also a culture that cultivated the lie that pornography was normal. Let me tell you a secret . . . it's not. At times, I felt like I wasn't a wife, I was a possession. This belief only fuelled my insecurities and caused me to retreat even further into myself.

We muddled through until that marriage also ended in divorce. In the end, our differences were too great and our issues too deep. My husband's reliance on pornography had become untenable for me, and when I asked him to get rid of his collection, it was as though I had asked him to cut off his arm. He still held the belief that it was a healthy part of a sexual relationship and subsequently accused me of not valuing our marriage. He called me a prude and accused me of not being adventurous or 'spicy' enough. We were on completely different wavelengths, and it eventually became an insurmountable source of contention between us. With nothing of substance really holding us together, it was probably inevitable that the marriage would fall apart sooner or later.

$$\sim$$

It's easy to see how unresolved pain and insecurity from our past can create unhealthy choices which influence our future. I'm not typically an advocate of the generational cycle, where people try to excuse their behaviour as an adult by blaming things they observed and experienced as a child. As a trained counsellor, I know there are genuine mental health and physical issues which persevere into adulthood and require professional intervention. That's not what I'm talking about, and I am in no way minimising those very real issues. However, people often get stuck in a victim mentality and think they, or their circumstances, can't ever change. It only takes one person to rise up with courage and faith, and say, "Enough is enough! My past will no longer negatively influence me or my relationships."

While I do acknowledge that my experiences as a young child and teenager did profoundly influence my beliefs and behaviour, I am not going to lay blame on anyone. I am a survivor, yes. But I refuse to be a victim. I reject the victim card, and I refuse to let it define my life.

There is a beautiful story in the Bible about a man named Joseph. He suffered betrayal and injustice for much of his life, yet right at the very end, he said of those who mistreated him:

> *"You intended to harm me, but God intended it all for good.*
> *He brought me to this position so I could save the lives of*
> *many people."*
>
> Genesis 50:20, NLT

Joseph was able to understand how the difficult circumstances of his life could be used for the good of others. Our own testimony can encourage others to do the same. There are people who need to hear your story—people who are going through what you've been through whose lives can be changed by what you have to share. How I wish someone with a similar story had come alongside me to guide and mentor me in those early years!

CHAPTER EIGHT

The God-Factor

One of the contributing factors to the end of my marriage was a radical encounter I had with God. It was so radical, in fact, that my life took a complete 180-degree turn.

I guess you could say I was raised in a 'Christian home'. Although my dad seldom attended church, my mum faithfully took me and my brothers. I went to Sunday School and youth group, which was where I also experienced my first 'crush' and suffered my first broken heart through unrequited puppy love. When I was old enough, I went through the ritual of Confirmation and took Holy Communion, but while I had lots of head knowledge *about* God, I lacked heart knowledge *of* God. When I was about twelve years of age, I responded to an altar call and committed to following Jesus. At the time, my belief was genuine. However, I was quickly drawn away from my new-found faith by the pull of the world. I was more interested in trying to be part of the 'cool crowd' than I was about anything else—though I never did quite make it despite my best efforts!

I carried this head knowledge of God into adulthood, and if you had asked me, I would have called myself a Christian. I went to church most Sundays and I even attended a small home group. Outwardly I was doing all the 'right' things, but I was privately holding onto so much ugliness in my life. I was bitter and unforgiving of those who had hurt me.

Now it was different. I'd had a defining moment of realisation that I couldn't hide who I really was from God. He knew everything about me, including the fact that my 'public' life was so very different from the life I lived behind closed doors. I felt so naked in my shame. I felt vulnerable in the knowledge that I could no longer live in denial about my life choices. It was time to get real with myself and stop pretending. I needed to stop playing the part of being a Christian and start actually living like one. For the first time in my life, I understood the difference between knowing about God and having a relationship with Him. This, I realised, was what I had been looking for all along.

~

This change in perspective was the catalyst I needed to finally confront the simmering problems in my marriage. My lifestyle was so messed up, and I realised I had compromised so much of my authentic self in my desperate need to be loved and accepted. I knew the way I was living was wrong, and I repented—which simply means to change your mind. Gradually I began to change, and I realised I had been holding on to so much bitterness and anger over things that had happened in my past. The reality of Matthew 6:15 hit home and shook me to my core:

"But if you do not forgive others their sins, your Father will not forgive your sins."

This is such a powerful scripture. Forgiveness is not a choice we get to make; it is a command we are told to obey. If I don't forgive others, God won't forgive me. In Ephesians 4:32, we also read,

"Be kind and compassionate to one another, forgiving each other, just as in Christ God forgave you."

Some versions of this passage use the word tender-hearted. I love that as it offers a whole new perspective on the people who have hurt me. It is impossible to stay mad at someone when you perceive them with a tender heart. Try it.

I remember pleading with God at the time not to turn His back on me. I was so messed up and convinced I had bought myself a one-way ticket to Hell. I believed I had done way too many bad things to ever be worthy of Heaven, and I begged God to find at least one redeeming quality in me to work with. I even tried bargaining with Him. Of course, there was no bargaining to be done. God is sovereign, and He doesn't bargain. Yet He was so merciful in His kindness toward me and was never going to turn His back on me! Another favourite scripture of mine is Isaiah 42:3,

> *"He will not crush the weakest reed or put out a flickering candle.*
> *He will bring justice to all who have been wronged." (NLT)*

Even at our lowest points, He is always there.

~

I think my ex was challenged by the 'new me' as I began to attend church more regularly and became more involved. After sharing my story at a women's event, I was invited to start a small group for women, many of whom had experienced childhood abuse similar to me. I was growing in who I was, and I was getting stronger and more confident in who I was becoming. This new-found sense of worth was unfamiliar territory for me. I drew closer to God than I ever had before and found a strength I did not know I had. A short time later I would have to draw on every ounce of that strength when my ex-husband ended our marriage, ironically by running off with someone else and having an affair. It was the very thing he had spent our entire marriage telling me I would do to him.

He justified the affair by saying that I was spending too much time 'trying to save the world' and that I no longer had enough time for him and his needs. That, and I had let myself go. I was 'too busy' and 'too fat'. Neither could have been further from the truth, still it is always easier to blame the other person than to take responsibility for yourself. It's one of the downfalls of human nature. We don't want to be accountable for our actions; we'd rather have a scapegoat take the blame on our behalf.

He finally told me he didn't love me anymore and wanted to separate as we were driving home from an interstate family wedding. Maybe it's just me, but I reckon driving down the freeway at one hundred and ten kilometres an hour might not be the most appropriate time to drop such a surprise revelation. It's possibly only by the grace of God that either of us survived the rest of that trip home.

∼

Despite everything, I tried in vain to save my marriage. I think this was partly because somewhere deep inside I still loved him, but also because I was dumbstruck that this could have happened again. I was so ashamed that my second marriage had ended that I didn't tell anyone for weeks. *What kind of failure must I be to have two marriages end in divorce?* I was both mortified and devastated. *What is wrong with me?* I wondered. *Am I really that unlovable? Am I really that hard to live with? Am I really that unworthy? Am I really that ugly?* Every negative emotion I had ever felt throughout my life came rushing back to the surface.

The worst thing you can do in times like this is to isolate yourself from your friends and support network. Unfortunately, it's also the very thing we usually end up doing, and it's exactly what I did. I did not go to church for fear that people would ask innocent questions about my husband that I was not ready or able to answer. However, you can't hide under a rock forever, as appealing as the thought sometimes seems! I very nearly lost my identity and my mind, but for God and a handful of wonderful friends who helped me slowly gain it back. I can't overemphasise how important it is to surround yourself with good people who will love you, keep you accountable, and encourage you to get back up and keep going when it's the last thing you want to do. They will shine light and love into the dark and hurting recesses of your heart, and when you feel like you're sinking, they will be your lifeline through the storm.

The Bible talks often about close friendships. One example is in Exodus 17:12 when two of Moses' close friends, Aaron and Hur, hold his hands up during battle:

> *"When Moses' hands grew tired, they took a stone and put it under him and he sat on it. Aaron and Hur held his hands up— one on one side, one on the other—so that his hands remained steady till sunset."*

This is a great example of what good friends do—they hold our hands and keep us strong when we can't do it on our own.

～

From the time my ex-husband's affair was exposed to the time he finally left for good was around six months. It felt more like six years. For six months, I fought for my marriage. For six months I endured so much emotional torture that at times I doubted I would ever recover. For six months I was so focussed on fixing 'us' that I completely forgot about 'me'. My ex and I both carried an enormous amount of baggage into our marriage, and we ultimately collapsed under its weight. I can't say whether things would have been different if we had dealt with our respective issues. Maybe our marriage would have ended anyway, but it may not have ended quite so catastrophically.

When it became obvious that the marriage was over, I invited my husband's girlfriend out for coffee—yes, I really did. I want to say my motives for doing this were totally pure. It would be nice to be able to say I was the better person and took the higher ground, but it wouldn't be totally true. Even though a part of me genuinely did want to show her grace and forgiveness, a bigger part of me just wanted to know why.

To her credit and my surprise, she accepted my invitation. And while she could not answer my question, we ended up having a surprisingly good chat. Ironically, in another time or place, I think we could have been quite good friends. Ultimately, I forgave them both, wished them well, and started to move on with my life.

CHAPTER NINE

Healing from Divorce

Healing from adultery and divorce is a complex maze to navigate. I think sometimes people see divorce as an easy way out. The mantra is, "Oh well, it didn't work, I should just give up and find someone else to make me happy." But it doesn't work like that. Divorce is hard on everyone involved. And the grass is not always greener on the other side.

Anyone who says divorce only affects two people is kidding themselves. Children, grandparents, extended family and even friends are all hugely impacted by the breakdown of a marriage. There is collateral damage on innocent bystanders, and broken relationships that sometimes never recover.

The following list is by no means exhaustive, but I have included some key points to consider as you move through the various stages of healing from a divorce. I have drawn on my personal experiences and most of my advice in this section is quite generic. However, if you are in, or escaping from, an abusive or dangerous relationship, please seek help from professionals. You and your children's safety should always be your top priority.

1. Give Yourself Time

Be kind to yourself. You don't have to have all the answers, and there is no appropriate timeframe for 'getting over' the breakdown of your relationship. It's different for everyone and no one should tell you otherwise. If, however, you're still stuck and unable to move on with your life after many years, it might be time to get some therapy. Be prepared to run the gamut of emotions: shock, anger, sadness, denial . . . and ultimately, acceptance. These are all perfectly normal reactions to what you've been through, and you will likely experience all of them—probably more than once.

There will be times when you thought you had moved through a stage only for something to trigger memories and cause the hurt to come flooding back. This can happen a lot in the first year when everything is the 'first anniversary' of doing things on your own, but sometimes these emotions can surface even years later. Don't feel like you have to rush into a new relationship either. Allow yourself the time and space to adjust and start the healing process before making any major life changes. This is especially important if you have children as they need to be given stability at a time when their world is probably falling apart as well.

2. Stay Connected

It is so important that you don't isolate yourself. You don't have to be alone in this—reach out and accept help. Find a good friend or mentor who will be honest with you, even when you don't want to hear it, and allow them to speak into your life. But be careful to avoid surrounding yourself with unhelpful people who can be quick to take you down a path you don't want to go down. Misery loves company, and it will be helpful to set healthy boundaries around yourself as you heal.

3. Know Your Rights

Don't make the mistake of thinking that even if you separate on amicable terms, the relationship will stay that way. There are always some extraordinary exceptions, but you don't want to discover this when it is already too late. I'm not trying to be negative or scare you; I'm just being realistic based on my own experience and that of others I know. Family law differs from place to place, so be sure to do your research. Most importantly, never allow anyone to make you feel guilty for protecting yourself, your assets, and your relationship with your children.

4. Allow Yourself to Grieve

Grief is a vital part of the healing process. You are not a superhero or a martyr, and it's important to give yourself permission to feel and express your emotions. You have not only lost an intimate relationship, but you've also lost family relationships and, more than likely, friends as well. You will also deeply feel the loss of hopes and dreams once intrinsically linked to those people and relationships. And you will need time to process the loss of your identity, especially if your spouse has blamed you for the breakdown of the relationship.

5. Forgive

This is probably the most difficult step in the whole process but also the most important, especially if you've been betrayed. Without forgiveness, you will be unable to move forward and will likely remain stuck in emotional bondage to your former partner. It is often said that unforgiveness chains you to your past, poisons your present, and keeps you from your future. This is very true, but forgiveness is also a biblical command. Matthew 6:14-15 says:

"For if you forgive other people when they sin against you, your heavenly Father will also forgive you. But if you do not forgive others their sins, your Father will not forgive your sins."

Unforgiveness will keep you bitter and will ultimately destroy you. It will make you sick and will negatively influence all your other relationships. It can be a daily struggle, especially if your former partner is exhibiting no remorse or still trying to make your life difficult. You may never get the apology or even the explanation you so desperately crave but that shouldn't and mustn't stop you from forgiving them. Forgiveness is the only action that will truly set you free and allow you to move on.

6. Parent As Well As You Can

This one is a minefield. There are times where a former partner has become so bitter, they do everything they can to sabotage the relationship between their children and the other parent. While doing this may make you feel better by venting and appearing to be the 'favourite' or 'better' parent, you are unfairly giving your child a warped view of the other parent and ultimately denying them a proper and healthy relationship with them. This may sound appealing in the short term, but it could come back to bite you when your children later learn the truth. It often puzzles me when people become so bitter after a breakup that they make out there was never any love or happiness in the relationship. If you never loved them, why were you with them in the first place? In my opinion, saying things like that only makes you sound foolish.

If you have a fractured relationship with the other parent of your children, please understand your issue is with your ex-partner, not their parents or extended family. Your children are not commodities or pawns to be used against your former partner or their family. You may not want to have anything to do with each other, but your children did not make that choice and you have to be responsible and put your feelings aside for the sake of ongoing healthy parent and child relationships.

~

There is much more I could say on this topic, but I think it can really be summed up in two words: be kind. Be kind to yourself, to your children, and to your former partner—and if you can't be kind to them, at least try to be kind about them. So much unnecessary heartache could be avoided if people stopped turning their relationships into a competition which no one ends up winning, and focused instead on what is best for everyone involved.

CHAPTER TEN

New Beginnings

The interesting thing about healing is that one day you get out of bed, dust yourself off, and realise that life goes on. For me, this 'aha moment' was actually a tangible thing. I remember talking with my son one day and laughing at something he said. I didn't think anything of it until he commented that it was the first time he'd heard me laugh in a long time. It was true; I had recovered my joy. More than that, I was no longer dwelling on the past but was content with life. It didn't really make sense, but I was at peace—the kind of peace that we read about in Philippians 4:7 that surpasses understanding:

> *"Then you will experience God's peace, which exceeds anything*
> *we can understand. His peace will guard your hearts and minds*
> *as you live in Christ Jesus." (NLT)*

I had been on my own for about a year by this point, and I was quite happy in my singleness. I was healthy in body, mind, and spirit; I looked good, and I felt great. I was travelling more and doing many things I had always wanted to do but had never been able to. In fact, I would say I was probably in the best place I had ever been in my life. I certainly wasn't interested in looking for a new relationship. It was actually nice to not be accountable to another person and to make decisions for myself for a change. Then, God decided to throw me another curve ball, only this time it was one I was more than happy to catch.

~

On the anniversary of the date my previous marriage had ended, I wrote a 'wearing my heart on my sleeve' kind of Facebook post that went something like this:

> *For 365 days, I have survived, and I have thrived. Thank you to everyone who has walked beside me and even carried me on this journey during the past year.*

It was important for me to say a genuine and heartfelt thanks to the people who had supported me and walked through the valley with me. After posting it, I received lovely words of encouragement and love. There were lots of public comments I would have expected from my friends . . . and one private inbox message that took me completely by surprise and came from the last person I would have ever expected to hear from.

James and I attended the same church although we didn't move in the same social circles and knew each other by name and sight only. We were both 'newly single' having been on the wrong end of infidelity in our previous marriages. Interestingly, we were already Facebook friends, but to this day, neither of us remember how that happened. Maybe it was divine intervention.

After reading his message of encouragement, I sent one back, not wanting to appear rude. The very next day there was another message in my inbox, and again I replied. My young adult son thought it was hilarious, saying, "This guy is hitting on you!" Of course, I denied it, and I'm sure it wasn't the intent of the original message, but it was still good to hear after my ego had been so bruised and battered during my divorce. Yet a pattern was forming, and unbeknown to both of us at the time, it was the beginning of our beautiful story of redemption.

The circumstances that brought James and I together could only have been orchestrated by a loving God who knew us both intimately and what each of us needed in a life partner. We had both been deeply wounded by unfaithful ex-spouses, and we initially connected through a profound level of understanding that comes through shared experiences.

That first Facebook message started a two-month long series of back-and-forth communication. These conversations slowly became less about the pain we had experienced and more about the beautiful new beginning that was unexpectedly unfolding before us. From behind the safety of our computer screens, we chatted about anything and everything, and this was the only interaction we had for several months. Despite seeing each other at church almost every Sunday, we were too shy to speak to each other in person! We were like a couple of awkward teenagers basking in the wonder of a new emerging love. It was very cute.

~

Just over two months after sending that first message, James simultaneously invited me out for coffee *and* gave me his phone number so I could reply via text. Until this point, our communication had been exclusively online so my brain almost exploded as I considered this latest development. *What if I say yes? What if I say no? If I send him a text, he will have my phone number. Do I want him to have my phone number?!?!*

Here I was, a grown woman in her forties, agonising over whether to go out for a coffee date! The beautiful innocence of it all still makes me smile, and I remember my work friend laughing at me as we sat in my office while I stressed over what to do. I guess I knew even then that this was never going to be just a coffee. Our first date lasted for over two hours and only ended because the café was closing for the day. Completely oblivious to the fact that we were the only ones left sitting there, we obviously had lots to talk about!

Our second date was the following Sunday. We had an in-person conversation in the car park after church (which, I might add, sent the church rumour mill into overdrive!) and decided to go out for lunch. We got hamburgers from my local takeaway and sat on the riverbank where we talked freely and openly about the feelings we could sense developing between us. We knew this was more than just a blossoming friendship born out of shared experiences; by now it had become a fully-fledged romance. It was only when the hunger pangs started and the light began to fade that we realised we had been sitting there for hours. Lunch time had long since passed, and we had once again talked well into the early evening.

Even though we had both been married previously, we were experiencing feelings like neither of us had ever had before. I had spent most of my life believing I was ugly, but James was the first man who made me believe I was beautiful. I had been called many things by previous men, usually objectifying, crude and vulgar comments relating to certain aspects of my anatomy, but never 'beautiful'. The way he still looks at me with so much sincerity and love in his eyes, reminding me I am made in the image of God, makes my heart melt even now.

During our courtship, we would often ask ourselves, "Is this what falling in love is supposed to feel like?" We knew very quickly we were meant to be together and were married within twelve months of our first date. Our engagement only lasted four months—barely enough time to plan a wedding!

CHAPTER ELEVEN

A Marriage Made in Heaven

James and I wanted to be together as soon as possible. We couldn't see the sense in maintaining two separate households, but we didn't want to just move in and live together either. Given that our previous marriages had left us feeling used and cast aside, we made a promise to each other before God that we would abstain from a sexual relationship until we were married.

I know for many people this is considered an old-fashioned concept, but it was an important thing for us to do, particularly for me. Every other sexual experience in my life had derived from the expectation that sexual intimacy was designed for the man's pleasure only, and if I kept him happy, everything would be fine. But I wanted our 'first time' to be different. I wanted to experience the nervous anticipation of waiting, and more importantly, to know I was worth waiting for. Unlike in my previous marriage, I wanted to be treated like a precious gift to be enjoyed, not an object to be 'had'. Although it was difficult at times, the wait was absolutely worth it.

∼

I joked before about the church rumour mill going into overdrive when James and I first became a couple. Well, as you might imagine, it went into absolute meltdown when we announced we were getting married!

The church we attended at the time had been rocked by a series of marriage break-ups—all of them a result of adultery. Within a twelve-month period, at least five marriages broke down irretrievably including our respective former marriages. These were all people who were loved and respected in the church community, and in most cases no one would have suspected anything was wrong. They were marriages that appeared solid and happy until one partner just disappeared, often without explanation, leaving a trail of unanswered questions and devastated family and friends in their wake. In the resulting fallout, many happily married couples started questioning themselves. *If it can happen to them, can it happen to us, too?* Strong secure Christians suddenly started questioning the basis of their faith. The entire church grieved and mourned.

So, when we announced we were getting married, many people thought this was just the occasion to bring joy back into the church. Desperate for a big display of victory after so much disappointment, people felt emotionally invested in our situation. Unfortunately, this led to them feeling entitled to offer unsolicited advice on how, when and where our marriage ceremony should take place, and who should be invited. Our wedding plans became a free-for-all, and boundaries were often blurred or ignored. I was even told by a straight-talking friend that I was being selfish for not including everyone. Her words, although possibly well-meaning, stung and cut me to the core.

I like to think most people are generally well-intentioned, but even the most well-meaning advice can be misconstrued or unwarranted. Not everyone knows the intimate details of your life—nor should they. Oftentimes, people offer advice based on their perspective of how your life should look in accordance with their worldview. They may be uncomfortable with the fact that you've moved on, and they haven't, or unintentionally project their own pain onto you to make themselves feel better.

Those who were the most vocal concerning our wedding arrangements needed us to release them from the pain and hurt caused by the recent chaos within the church. Our wedding was the opportunity for them to finally move on. But, releasing them from their 'stuckness' was not our responsibility; it was theirs. We couldn't heal their pain for them—only God can do that. It would have been impossible and foolish for us to even try. We quickly realised we were never going to please everyone, nor did we want to.

This was our day, and the joy we felt was fast becoming tarnished. In a spur-of-the-moment decision, we cancelled the plans we had already made and decided to have a small, intimate beach wedding two hours away, with only a handful of close family and friends in attendance. We had both done the 'big wedding' extravaganza before, and neither of us had any need or desire to do it again. I know we would have regretted bowing to the pressure of orchestrating a big production neither of us wanted. Our day ended up being perfect; we held our ceremony at a place that was very special to me on a beautiful and unusually warm winter's day.

~

Looking back, our beautiful love story is living proof that when you put your faith in God, things have a way of turning out for the best. As it says in Romans 8:28:

"And we know that in all things God works for the good of those who love him, who have been called according to his purpose."

There have been so many twists and turns in my journey that it sometimes makes my head spin. Yet, James and I often remind one another to embrace the detours when they come because they almost always come with a purpose. No matter what obstacles, challenges or disappointments come our way, we always have a choice in how to respond to them. You can let them make you, or you can let them break you, and I've found that life is far more enjoyable when viewed from a glass-half-full perspective!

For the first ten years of our marriage, we faced what seemed like insurmountable obstacles. Being vulnerable enough to trust again after divorce is hard. James and I have faced many challenges as we have navigated some very difficult waters. But we have also had some incredible and joyous moments. We dared to dream and have worked hard to make those dreams come true. In doing so, we have achieved more than we ever thought possible.

$$\sim$$

At one point during the early months of our blossoming friendship, James casually commented that if we were both still single in a few years' time we should meet up at the Eiffel Tower. I jumped on it like a dog with a bone, and from that moment on, it became a standing joke that he had invited me to dine at the Eiffel Tower. He insisted that's not what he meant but I had no intention of ever letting him forget it! We never did give up on that dream, and in 2017—the year of our 5th wedding anniversary and our combined fiftieth birthdays—we went to Paris and had that dinner. It was everything I had ever dreamed it would be. As we sat down at our table overlooking the lights of the city below, I'm not ashamed to admit my eyes may have leaked a bit as the reality of the moment hit home. I hope it inspires you to never give up on your dreams. They are worth fighting for.

Another significant moment in our marriage was the day we received the Certificate of Occupancy for our house. When James and I first started dating, he invited me over to his house to show me what I was getting into! To say the house was a mess would be the understatement of the century. It had been partially demolished and extended in readiness for a renovation before James was unceremoniously dumped and left with a massive building project and very few financial or practical resources to finish it. He had refinanced and bought the other share in the home as part of the divorce settlement because it was important to him to complete the project and provide his children with a secure home base. In all honesty, there was probably an element of him wanting to prove to the doubters that he could do it as well.

As I waded through the clutter, cautiously stepping over tools, building rubble, car bits, and the occasional dead rodent, I looked at the man standing next to me (who by now was probably very thankful I hadn't turned and run), and saw a vision of what this mess could one day look like. In that moment, I was sold.

One of the first things we did was to change the original renovation plans as I didn't want to build someone else's dream. It was important to both of us that this home became 'ours'. We were bound by some things we couldn't change, but for the most part, the house we have built is entirely different from what was originally planned. As I put my own personal touches on it, I often used the saying, 'turning a house into a home'. Even amidst the building chaos it was important to me that we created a welcoming space for our combined brood of seven offspring—along with two in-laws and grandchildren—to 'come home to'.

By the time we received our Certificate of Occupancy, we had poured buckets of blood, sweat and tears into building a beautiful home. It was a laborious slog, and on more than one occasion, we nearly had to walk away due to the intense financial and emotional pressures we were under. But God has been so faithful to us. He has provided, sometimes miraculously, everything we have needed. Our story is proof that "with God nothing will be impossible" (Luke 1:37, NKJV).

When we were close to being finished, my friend Jossie gave me a handmade wooden chopping board that said, *"Mr. & Mrs. James and Vikki Southwell . . . turned a house into a home."* It remains one of my most treasured possessions and holds pride of place in my kitchen as a precious reminder of the fulfilment of our dream.

CHAPTER TWELVE

A Time of Transition

Five years after we became a couple, James and I made the difficult decision to leave the church where we had first met. We had wanted to stay—it had been our church home for many years and we had persevered through many different seasons—but it was just too difficult. As our relationship unfolded, we felt like we were living in a fishbowl. Everybody knew our business, and while I appreciated their genuine but sometimes misguided interest in our emerging new beginning, it was suffocating us. We couldn't flourish as individuals or as a couple. And worse than that, I believe we had even started to go backwards. Ultimately, as much as we wanted to play a part in the emotional rebuilding of our church, it became impossible for us to remain there. It turned out to be the right decision for us—thirteen years later I still know of people who have been unable to let go and move on from that church's complicated history.

It was important to us to leave well, so we allowed a full twelve months to transition out while looking for a new church. I believe that when you leave a church, you shouldn't just 'disappear'. This is not only disrespectful to the leadership but can also be hurtful to people who have more than likely invested in you. It's always better to be honest, and disappearing without explanation can often cause more questions and room for speculation. It might not change anything, but at least if you leave following godly principles you can go with your head held high. Romans 12:18 says, "If it is possible, as far as it depends on you, live at peace with everyone." This means leaving well, as far as it depends on you, and also ensures that the door is not slammed shut if you ever want to return.

I understand this is not always possible, and I am sadly also fully aware that disrespect and hurt can just as easily come from within your church leadership. The Church is full of imperfect people, including pastors. A pastor can even be the reason a person leaves a church, sometimes with good cause. It's important, however, not to confuse your pastor with God. Church leaders are to be respected but not adored, and you should never put your pastor on a pedestal that is too lofty for them to maintain. The Church may be Christ's bride, but it is not God, and we should never blame Him for the actions of the Church or one of its representatives. It's important to remember that the Church didn't die for you, Jesus did. So, we should seek Him first, along with wise godly counsel, and if we still feel led to go, we should exit well, and go wherever He is leading us.

When we finally left, it was with the full support and blessing of the new pastors, who had also become our friends. God soon led us to the church where He already knew the next part of my story was about to evolve.

～

When we transitioned into our new church, we wanted to be Mr. and Mrs. Nobody for a while and allow ourselves to fully heal from what we had left behind. It was all going really well too—until the women's pastor invited me out for a coffee. We were having a lovely chat and getting to know one another when the inevitable point in the conversation came.

People have a natural curiosity to ask about your story when you first meet, especially in a church setting. I was prepared for that question and expecting it when she asked. We had come to the point where I could either take the conversation in a different direction, as I had done many times before when I didn't want to talk about it, or tell her the whole story. It seemed a natural choice to choose the latter.

As I started to explain our situation, she stopped me in my tracks with just two words: "I know." *What!? How could she possibly know why we had left our previous church?* Once I got over the shock, the question left my mind and came out of my mouth, "How do you know?"

It turned out that one of the assistant pastors at our new church, who already knew our story, felt it was important to share it with the rest of the staff. Although he felt he needed to be accountable to the leadership, and I understand that perhaps the senior pastor should be made aware of such things, I question if it was necessary for the entire staff to know everything. Your church is supposed to be a safe place to share your confidences without worrying whether it is going to be the topic of discussion at the next staff meeting! It wasn't life-threatening or soul-destroying information, and it didn't affect my salvation, which are all the reasons I would expect something to be disclosed. All I could see was that we were once again the subject of unwanted gossip. I was devastated and felt so let down.

We have a saying in Australia, "Not happy, Jan!" It comes from an advertising campaign in the early 2000's and is used when someone is extremely upset over something that someone else has done. It's a very funny ad; you should google it. But I digress. To say, "I was not happy, Jan" would be the understatement of the year. I wasn't just unhappy. I was furious!

This is an example of when Satan tries to prevail but God's will always wins. Through this, the devil tried to discourage and distract me from being in the very place God had prepared for me to be. I think the enemy knew the fruit that was going to come from my involvement with this church, so he used the apparent betrayal of a friend—the one thing he knew could cause me to drift off course. The reason the assistant pastor knew our situation better than most was not just because he attended our previous church during the tumultuous season of marriage break-ups; he was also a good friend of James' and knew intimate details of our story. I was shattered to think he had betrayed our confidence without even giving us the heads-up. I told James in no uncertain terms that I was never going back to that church!

James, however, was adamant we should give it another go. He is more practical than I am and could see immediately that there was no malice behind what was said. It was the truth. I knew the person involved was a nice guy who wouldn't deliberately hurt anyone. Still, I was being led by my emotions, and the following Sunday James had to drag me and my very ungracious attitude to church.

I made it very clear I didn't want to be there and stood through worship with my arms folded across my chest and a very unattractive scowl on my face. Anyone who knows me well knows that I typically cannot stand still if there is music playing, and no matter what I'm hearing, it is very out of character for me not to at least move to the beat. So, I must have been in a really bad mood! Then, God proved He was in control once again. It was time for the message, and guess who was preaching that morning! You got it, the assistant pastor. Not only had I been dragged to church, now I had to sit and listen to him preach! *Okay Lord,* I thought. *You've got my attention. I surrender.*

The truth is, if I had succumbed to my feelings and never gone back, I would never have been invited a couple of years later to join the staff as the new women's pastor and come face-to-face with my past. A new chapter was about to unfold.

CHAPTER THIRTEEN

Past and Present Collide

A baby dedication. At church, they happen all the time; it is a biblical principle to dedicate children to the Lord. And, as the women's pastor at the time, it was appropriate for me to present flowers and a children's Bible to the child's family. Just your average Sunday morning, nothing out of the ordinary here . . . An easy assumption to make, except on this Sunday, absolutely everything was out of the ordinary.

This was not just any baby dedication. In an extraordinary plot twist, the baby getting dedicated was the great-granddaughter of Jack's mother—the woman who had insisted I abort my first baby. Read that again. This baby girl would have been the second cousin of my baby. She was part of my history. This baby girl and my aborted baby, who her family would never know, biologically shared some of the same DNA. Not only that, but her entire family was there to witness the occasion, including Jack—the father of my baby—and his mother.

Then there was me. The skeleton they had tried to keep hidden in their closet for more than three decades was sitting in the middle of the front row, large as life. At that moment, my past and my present were colliding in the most spectacular way. I knew it, they knew it, and God knew it. Only the parents of the baby girl (who was blissfully unaware of all the drama surrounding her) did not know it.

I remember thinking at the time that only God would use a baby dedication to bring me, Jack and his mother together in the same room at the same time. To use the celebration of one life to acknowledge the death of another. The irony and poignancy of the moment was not lost on me.

~

Three years prior, I had been invited to join the church staff as the new women's pastor. I very quickly realised that one of my colleagues, Thomas, was the nephew of my baby's father, which made him my aborted baby's cousin. It was Thomas' baby getting dedicated, which is weird to think about, I know. I couldn't make this up if I tried!

I had picked up the connection almost immediately, but I kept it quiet for three years because I felt it was not my place to reveal his family secret . . . even though I was a colossal part of it! Eventually though, this knowledge started to burden me. I hate lies, and I hate having to keep secrets—unless it is a good one like a new puppy or something! The fact I worked with him and had to keep quiet about what I knew was increasingly difficult. Almost weekly, I would listen to him talk during our lunch breaks about his family. These were people I remembered all too well but I was unable to say anything to him.

Then, about eight months before the baby dedication, I made plans to have lunch with my good friend, Katie. We had changed the date, time and place of our lunch three times in the days leading up to it. Something always seemed to come up and force us to change our plans, and it was not long before I found out why. Little did I know then how pivotal this 'chance' encounter would prove to be.

You see, on that day, sitting at the table behind us was Jack's sister, the aunt of the baby I was forced to abort. As I write this, I hear a gentle but clear rebuke from the Holy Spirit: *Stop calling him that. The abortion is not his identity—or yours. You gave him a name; use it* . . . Yes, I did give him a name. His name is Michael.

Michael's aunt was sitting at the table behind us. Thankfully, I had my back to her, but I knew she was there and had great trouble concentrating on the conversation I was having. When my friend Katie said hello to her, my head went into a spin. *How do they know each other?!*

Outside the café, I could not contain myself any longer and asked her. Unaware of the weight behind my question, she casually replied, "We are family friends. We've known them for years." *Oh, boy.* I don't know whether it was because I was stunned or so on edge, but whatever the reason, the words started tumbling out of my mouth as I told her about the connection I had with this family.

For the first time, I was able to share my abortion story without being ambiguous about the other people involved. This story is about God's redemption in my life, and I have always been careful to protect the privacy of others. Still, on this occasion, it was entirely appropriate, and I believe God ordained it. Although I was shaking like a leaf as memories of that time in my life came flooding back, Katie knew precisely what to do and immediately spoke soothing words of affirmation over me and prayerfully ministered to my troubled soul. I would never have imagined in my wildest dreams that only eight months after that initial encounter, I would again be facing members of this family at, of all things, a baby dedication. But God . . .

~

Once I had established the connection between Jack's family and my friend, a whole lot of things began to happen. For the first time, I was confronted with the possibility of speaking to the person who had fathered then cruelly dismissed our child. I was not opposed to this idea and gave Katie's husband, Julian, permission to reach out to Jack on my behalf. *Surely, he would want to acknowledge and put our baby to rest as much as I did?*

Within days the answer had come back, and I once again felt the bitter sting of hurt, anger, and rejection. For thirty-six years, Jack had kept this part of his past a closely-guarded secret. Not even his wife knew about our unplanned teenage pregnancy and subsequent abortion, which in his words was "the right thing to do at the time because he didn't feel responsible enough to become a father." For all this time he had maintained his silence, and I daresay, his unresolved grief, and he was determined that now was *not* the time to bring it to the surface.

Wow, I sure did not see that coming. While I understood that having his past so abruptly and unexpectedly arrive in his present was no doubt confronting for him, I still could not understand how our baby could mean so little to him. Although I had forgiven him and his mother many years before, I could not stop the anger from rising within me. *You are nothing but a coward. How dare you be so dismissive?* My heart went straight into protection mode, and I thought it would end there. *Fine, if that's the way you want it, adios amigos.* Needless to say, God had other plans.

I used to wonder if Jack ever went on to have more children. I have since found out he didn't. I also can't help but wonder if he ever thinks about our baby. *Does he have any regret? Does he ever wonder what Michael might look like or what he might have done with his life?* Of course, I will probably never know the answers to these questions, and in the grand scheme of things it doesn't matter. Although my mother's heart does get curious sometimes as to whether there is even a hint of remorse from his perspective, ultimately it's none of my business what Jack thinks. It's tragic to reflect how choices like these can have such far-reaching and devasting consequences, not just in the lives of the people making those choices but also for so many others around them.

∼

I was sitting in my office at work when I received the confirmation from my friend Julian that the whole family, including Jack and his mother, would be attending the baby dedication a few weeks later. This news was not entirely unexpected because not only had the baby dedication been planned for weeks but I also knew the extended family was going to be in town for another event during the same weekend. Interestingly, the date of this event had been changed due to unexpected and unforeseen circumstances causing it to line up perfectly with the dedication. *Funny that.*

I knew then I had a choice to make—avoid or confront. With everything inside me balking at the idea, I chose to step up, put my big-girl panties on, and confront this looming encounter head-on. In the days leading up to the dedication, however, I would will myself to walk the few steps to my boss's office to ask him if I could bail out of church on Sunday. He knew my story and my connection with Jack's family, so he probably would have understood. But every time I tried to take a step, the Holy Spirit would stop me. Back and forth the conversation would go: *I can't do this. Yes, you can. No, I can't. Yes. You can.* Everyone knows you can't win an argument with God, but I still tried!

I kept hoping my boss would say something to get me off the hook, but I don't believe he even registered or thought about the connection until I raised it afterwards. I now know it was a good thing he didn't remember, because this was something I needed to face. Without this step forward, my story could not be complete. Internally I was a mess, and although I had a great support network, nobody fully understood what I was going through. I had nowhere to turn except to my Heavenly Father, who had clearly orchestrated this situation. I had no reason to believe He would not bring me through it, but that did not stop the anxiety from rising within me.

The night before the dedication, the realisation suddenly struck me that the following morning I would be walking onto the stage to present flowers and a Bible to people I would have been related to, had my baby been born. I would be face-to-face with a baby who shared some of the same DNA as Michael, and the eyes of the whole church would be watching all of this unfold, including Jack and his mother. The last time I felt this alone was in the abortion clinic connecting me to this family, and once again the irony was not lost on me.

I needed God now more than ever, and through tears of anguish I poured out my heart to Him. "I can't do this. I CANNOT DO THIS!" I cried out. *Yes, you can,* He replied. *You are not alone; I am with you. It's going to be okay. We've got this.* I was about to find out if He was right.

CHAPTER FOURTEEN

Facing My Giants

On the morning of the dedication, I planned how I would look to the nth degree. I was determined to prove to Jack's family that they had not destroyed me and that I was worthy of their respect. I especially wanted Jack's mother to see that I was good enough and would have ended up being 'acceptable' if she'd only given me a chance.

My grown-up self was going to bat for my sixteen-year-old self as I carefully chose my outfit and did my hair and makeup. On the outside, I was ready . . . but on the inside I was nowhere near. I was trembling but took comfort in the presence of James and our friends Katie and Julian who were the only other people in the room who knew exactly what was going on. Although I knew Jack had been given a heads-up from Julian that I would be there, I did not know for sure whether the rest of his family knew or if they would even recognise me. *Would they know who I was?*

As the band began to play the first song, *Raise a Hallelujah* by Bethel Music, I knew everything was going to be okay. The opening line talks about lifting your voice in worship in the presence of your enemies, and I have never related to a song more than I did at that moment. I sure was in the presence of my enemies; they were sitting just a few rows behind me! I have never leaned into worship more in my life than

I did that day. And I couldn't help but smile and laugh a little at the ridiculous irony of it all. For the first time in a long time, I was finally able to let out a long-held breath.

The service went off without a hitch, and afterwards Jack was hovering. I could see him out of the corner of my eye while I was mingling with other people, trying unsuccessfully to keep my mind occupied. It looked as though he wanted to speak to me but couldn't muster the nerve. What would he even say in this situation? *Nice weather today . . . How have you been since we killed our baby?* I had known Jack intimately and being so close to him after all this time was more than a little unnerving. I kept seeking out James' face across the crowd for reassurance.

As people started to leave, James and I were standing alone in the foyer. Looking up, I caught Jack's mother and sister looking and pointing at me from inside the auditorium. My earlier question about whether they would recognise me was answered in an unsettling instant. *They know.* I mustered every ounce of courage I had left to face them as they had no other option but to walk right past me on their way out. I was ready and willing to say hello.

In my imagination, I had played out this moment often over the past three decades. I naively envisioned a beautifully redemptive encounter filled with hugs, tears, and healing as Jack's mother apologised to me and asked for my forgiveness. But nothing could have prepared me for the harsh reality of her frosty silence and cold hard stare, piercing me to the very core of my being. Once again, she had made her thoughts about me crystal clear, and obviously I still wasn't worthy of her time or attention. The bitterness in her demeanour toward me was palpable, and as I watched her leave, I realised I'd had enough of being a big girl for one day. I was drained, and I needed to go home where it was safe.

When I reflected on it later, I was pleasantly surprised to realise I had faced my giants head-on only to discover they were nowhere near as big as I thought they were. The giants I had conjured up in my imagination were way bigger and scarier than the ones I encountered in real life. The experience taught me that life goes on and the past does sometimes come back to bite us, whether we're ready for it or not. I discovered that my worst enemy was myself, and I realised that despite the many scenarios that have played out in my mind over the years—both good and bad—people can only take up space in my head if I let them.

I lost a ton of emotional baggage that day when I fully understood it didn't matter anymore what Jack and his family thought of me. Their opinions of me carry no weight at all as my redemption is complete in the eyes of my Heavenly Father. I like to think He was proud of me as I trusted Him to get through what was, without doubt, one of the most difficult confrontations of my life. I could feel the weight lift as I realised it no longer mattered what other people's impressions were of me, especially those who are still weighed down by their own emotional baggage. From that day on, I was able to think of them with compassion instead of fear.

~

But while I had faced and defeated one set of problems, I had also created another. My story was something I could no longer keep hidden, and I felt it was time to come clean with my colleague Thomas about my connection to his family. I was torn between not wanting to hurt him but also knowing this was a secret that was ready to explode. Now that it had already started to trickle out, I could no longer risk him finding out from someone else, or worse, by me blurting something out during lunch one day. So, the Monday afternoon after the dedication, I found myself walking into my boss' office.

"Can we debrief the events of yesterday?" My boss looked up from his desk with a quizzical look on his face that clearly indicated he had absolutely no idea what I was talking about. I pressed further: "The baby dedication? The family connection?" His face lit up like a hundred-watt lightbulb had just illuminated his mind "Oh . . . Jack!" *Yes, Jack, and his mother, and the rest of the extended family.* "Right," he said. "Let's debrief. Tomorrow morning first thing."

My boss was the senior pastor of our church. He is also my colleague's father-in-law. He knew the details of my story because when I was applying for my pastoral credential, I had to disclose anything that might reflect poorly on the church. While I didn't think my powerful testimony of healing should trigger any negative feedback, I still felt it was important to share the truth about what I had been through. In a sense, I guess I wanted him to know what he was getting into with this women's pastor and give him an 'out' if he felt it was too much. Looking back, I don't really know why I would have thought that. After all, isn't it the truth that sets us free?

With James by my side, I had shared my story. I left nothing out, including the fact that the boy who got me pregnant at sixteen was my colleague Thomas' uncle. *Surprise!* My boss was very pragmatic about my confession, and it was never mentioned again . . . until now. Sitting in his office, we tried to figure out the best way for me to come clean to Thomas. It was a decision I agonised over. On the one hand, I felt strongly that I needed to be honest with him, but on the other hand, I was acutely aware that telling him could cause him pain and possibly damage relationships within his family. I was also, perhaps selfishly, very aware that I was opening myself up to further judgement. In the end, the reasons to speak up far outweighed the reasons to stay silent. I was ready and willing to take the risk. It was absolutely the right time to bring the truth into the open. But, how?

~

We decided the best course of action was to share a meal together. When all else fails, we eat! So James and I, along with Thomas and his wife, were invited to dinner at my boss' house. Only James, me and my boss knew the bombshell I was about to drop. The other three guests at this peculiar dinner party were completely oblivious and had no clue what was going on. I knew what I needed to say, I knew I had to say it, but I had no idea *how* to say it. I simply had to trust that God would give me the words when the time came. I also had to trust that He would give the others the grace to receive the story I was about to tell them.

I offered up a last-minute prayer, *God please be in the midst of this conversation and bring wisdom and soft hearts,* and with the knowledge that our friends were also praying on my behalf, I finally told Thomas the truth about Michael—the cousin he would never know. Through tears, I explained my relationship with his uncle, his grandmother's reaction to my pregnancy, and our decision to have an abortion. Thomas' response was reassuringly beautiful and will remain private. While obviously taken aback, he was very gracious. We didn't talk at length about the details—that would come later. I had already given the poor guy enough to process for one night!

When you walk in the dark, you are afraid of stumbling or tripping over, but when you turn on the light and see clearly, the fear is gone. Similarly, secrets lose their power when they're brought out into the open, into the light. When I revealed my secret to Thomas, it lost its hold over me, and for the first time in a long time, the heaviness in my spirit was gone. This feeling is described perfectly in Proverbs 28:13:

> *"Whoever conceals their sins does not prosper, but the one who confesses and renounces them finds mercy."*

Thomas' extended family are slowly becoming aware of this chapter in their history. From what I've heard, the reactions are mostly ambivalent. While I suspect they would prefer to remain ignorant of the details, I can't do that. The truth had to start somewhere, and I know God will use this situation for His glory and to bring much needed healing to a broken family. This is, and always has been, my prayer for them.

CHAPTER FIFTEEN

Freed to Forgive

The overarching theme throughout my life has been the need for forgiveness. Time and again, I have had to make the difficult choice to forgive others, and in some cases, this is an ongoing process. I have had moments of thinking, *Really, again?*, and this can be especially hard when there is no apparent repentance or remorse in response.

I know there are some wounds that are so deep-rooted and painful it is overwhelming to even acknowledge them, let alone forgive them. I know this because I have been there. I am not asking you to do something that can't be done. I have done it, and if I can do it, so can you. When I have at times been incapable of offering forgiveness in my own strength, praise God, I didn't have to. Since Christ paid the price of our sins on the cross, the work has already been done. We simply have to accept His grace and follow His example. It helps me to forgive others when I acknowledge the extent of the forgiveness I too have received.

If, while reading this, you feel moved to action, I urge you to take a step forward in your journey of forgiveness. I do not promise a quick fix, but I can tell you that if you allow God to do the work with you and in you, you will experience a transformation you won't believe is possible. At first, it might come through tears and gritted teeth, and that's okay. We all have to start somewhere—the important thing is to make a start. It's like riding a bike; the more you practice, the easier it becomes. And if you fall—and you will, because we're only human after all—simply pick yourself up and start again.

The person who has needed the most forgiveness over the years is me. Often, we can be our own worst enemy and harshest critic, punishing ourselves for things we have done wrong and rehashing past mistakes. Forgiving myself is hard—in my experience, it has always been easier to forgive others—but I have found it helpful to personalise the scripture from Ephesians 4:32:

> "Be kind and compassionate [to myself], forgiving [myself], just as in Christ God forgave [me]."

This exercise can give you a whole new perspective. Be kind to yourself. Show compassion to yourself. Stop beating yourself up. God loves you; Christ died for you. You are so worth it!

~

I believe there are far too many people burdened by choices and consequences from their past who need to encounter the saving grace of Jesus Christ. This is the only way we can step out of our internal prison into the freedom to be who we were truly created to be. In Jesus we are free to stop floundering from one unwise and desperate choice to the next without ever really going anywhere. We are free to stop searching for something without really knowing what we're looking for.

It is my opinion that if people were encouraged from an earlier age to find their identity in the One who created them, they wouldn't make so many unwise choices. If more young people understood how truly priceless they are and were taught to value themselves and their bodies instead of carelessly giving such a precious part of themselves away, there would be much less heartache and pain for future generations.

We need to raise our sons and daughters to treat each other with respect and to expect nothing less in return. I wish someone had drummed this wisdom into me when I was younger because I know what it feels like to carry the heavy weight of shame around. But if by sharing my story and pointing others to the love and forgiveness of Christ, I make a difference in someone's life, it will have been worth it.

CHAPTER SIXTEEN

Looking Forward with Hope

I have lost count of the number of times I have written the final chapter of this book in my head. It is my deepest desire that Michael's life was not snuffed out in vain and that his story would serve a greater purpose. Ever since I experienced my own healing from the abortion, I have prayed for an outcome that would bring forgiveness, restoration and healing for everyone else involved. And when the connection was discovered between my friends and Jack's family, I believed this would be it—an opportunity for Jack and me to acknowledge a life that would never be lived this side of Heaven and finally lay Michael to rest.

Unfortunately, Jack has yet to show any interest in confronting this situation and to give our baby the acknowledgement he deserves. It would appear he is still unwilling or unable to admit and accept the consequences of his actions, and I cannot put all my hope in a reconciliation that may never come. While I must end my story without the closure I had hoped for, God is not letting me end it without hope. Let me tell you why.

~

When I first felt the call back in 2007 to share my story and bring hope to women who had experienced similar situations, I was forced to confront my role in the abortion for the first time. It took more than twenty years for me to find forgiveness and healing from that time in my life. For more than two decades, I struggled in unhealthy relationships, desperately searching for something I could not even put into words. I finally realised the One I was searching for was Jesus. He knew me better than I knew myself because He created me, and He was the one Person I could cling to when everything else was falling apart.

I was just about to turn forty, and I couldn't help but see the comparison with the Israelites in the Old Testament who had wandered for forty years before entering the Promised Land. As with the Israelites, what I was looking for was right in front of me the whole time, it just took me far too long to realise it! I thank God He never gave up on them—or me. He won't give up on you either.

Perhaps you are still wandering in the desert, wanting desperately to move forward but unable to let go of the past. The first step is always the hardest because often we don't know where it will lead. The unknown can be a scary place, but I have found that God will give us everything we need to keep walking if we will only trust Him. He knows where we are going, even if we don't. Don't be like the generation of Israelites who were too afraid and too comfortable with the familiar (even though the familiar was not that comfortable!) that they never entered the Promised Land. For much of the time they wanted to go back rather than face the difficult process of moving forward. As a result, a whole generation of people died before receiving the life God had promised them. Even their leader, Moses, had to die before those who were left could receive what God had promised them.

Is there anything in your life that needs to die for you to move forward into the life you were created for? Please don't wait until it's too late to unburden yourself from the hurt, bitterness and unforgiveness from your past. I also want to encourage you, if you don't already know

Jesus as your Lord and Saviour, to consider asking Him into your life. Let me tell you, life with Him is so much better than life without Him. If you have felt a stirring to do this, don't ignore it; it's the Holy Spirit reaching out to you. Jesus loves you and only wants the best for you. There doesn't have to be any fuss or fanfare; a simple prayer confessing your sin, asking for forgiveness, and inviting Him to come into your life to walk with you and guide you from now on is all you have to do. It really is that simple. Please reach out if you've already taken that step. I'd love to hear about it!

~

As part of my healing journey, God, in His infinite mercy, showed me a tender vision of my child growing up in Heaven—a boy with dark, curly ringlets. I have held this precious image close to my heart, not sharing it with anyone except my mum. It comforts me to know that my boy went straight from my womb into the arms of Jesus.

In my humanness, I have sometimes found myself wondering if this vision was just a figment of my imagination, a desperate attempt to justify my actions. And even if it was, it would have still given me incredible hope. But I now know that isn't the case. One day, when my friends Julian and Katie were praying for me, Julian said he saw a vision of my child. He went on to describe him to me—right down to his dark, curly ringlets. This is information Julian could never possibly have known, so I am left in no doubt that God is real, God is faithful, and God is looking after my son until I get the chance to meet him myself. If you are the mother or father of an aborted child, I pray this brings peace to your heart, too. Your child is in Heaven, and you will get to meet them one day.

While the final closure I had hoped and prayed for hasn't yet happened, I am not ruling it out. Perhaps my story will have a sequel where true healing in Jack's family can take place, forgiveness will be offered and received, and Jack and I will finally lay our baby to rest. I can only imagine what that moment might feel like. For now, it seems like an impossibility. But I have no doubt that in God's timing, nothing is impossible.

~

Oh and the baby girl whose dedication brought this final chapter into the light? I can't tell you her name, but I can tell you it means dawn, white (pure), or bright. Her middle name means hope. A dawn of pure, bright hope . . . how wonderfully and beautifully appropriate.

Epilogue

Writing this book has been a very therapeutic process. It is an amazing story of God's redeeming grace, and even though publishing it is a terrifying step, I know this is what I have been called to do. We can all make an impact in the lives of those around us, and I hope to leave a positive legacy for the generations still to come.

Despite what I've been through, I have chosen to make the best of situations and rely on God for my direction and provision. Do I have regrets? Not really. While the situations I have been through and the choices I have made have led to incredible pain, hurt, and disappointment, I can't live with regret. I believe life is too short to live with crippling regrets that weigh you down and hold you back. Living with regret would also mean I have not been fully restored in Jesus Christ. He died for the redemption of my sins—all of them. So, holding onto regret is, in a way, saying that what He did for me was not enough.

It was. In fact, it was more than enough and way more than I deserved. I have been blessed with my husband James—an amazing man who is living proof that God really does save the best until last. I have a wonderful family and some beautiful friends. My abortion experience has been redeemed in a way I could never have imagined in my wildest dreams. Although painful at the time, it ultimately led to the birth of my two children who I absolutely adore and cannot imagine being without. It was in them that I finally found what true love looked like. And while life has not always gone in the direction I would have liked, I have still been given many opportunities for which to be grateful. I refuse to be a victim and let what has happened to me define me. I refuse to let my past dictate my future. My identity is not wrapped up in where I've been; it is beautifully focused on where I'm going.

I am still a work in progress. I don't always get it right, and I still make mistakes. The point is this: Bad things sometimes happen to good people and good people sometimes do bad things. We are never going to get it exactly right this side of Heaven, but we all have a choice in whether our circumstances make us or break us. I now know the richness and fullness of a life with Christ in comparison to the emptiness of a life without Him. Romans 8:37 says,

> "... in all these things we are more than conquerors through
> him who loved us."

I said before that my story contained more twists and turns than a rollercoaster in a theme park. It hasn't always been an easy ride, but I have learned to enjoy it, because of the One who rides beside me. My journey has at times been difficult, but I can now look back and see that I was never alone. Even when I did not acknowledge Him, God has been there beside me every step of the way working out my circumstances for good. Now, I can see that He is placing the final pieces in a puzzle that was once a jumbled mess of brokenness but is now an exquisitely crafted masterpiece.

Appendix: A Journey to Healing

This *Journey to Healing* tool contains ten practical steps relating to the areas I believe most commonly hold people back in their efforts to move forward after trauma. This material began as notes for a small group I was running for women in the church I was attending at the time; however, every week as I prepared to lead the group, my notes tended to morph, until eventually I developed them into a ten-part course for personal healing.

In each of the following ten sections we will address the key issues I believe keep us bound to our past, and then learn to let them go and leave them where they belong. At the end of each section there are questions for you to answer. I encourage you to be honest with your answers and to be ready to receive what God wants to say to you. Together let's learn to appreciate who we are in Christ, discover strength we didn't know we had, and start walking toward the incredible and wonderful future God has planned for us.

I pray you will be blessed as you take this journey!

1

Leaving the Past Behind

Often it is our mindset or beliefs that keep us from moving forward. Perhaps you have found yourself saying:

My past determines my future.
I am who I am because of my circumstances.
I cannot change anything.
This is my lot in life . . . I don't deserve any better.

While this might feel true, the fact is, God says your future is bright! Yes, your past has certainly shaped who you are, but it must not be allowed to define you. God wants to turn your past experiences into an opportunity to help others. Let's allow God to turn our lemons into lemonade!

Forget the former things; do not dwell on the past. See, I am
doing a new thing! Now it springs up; do you not perceive it? I
am making a way in the desert and streams in the wasteland.
Isaiah 43:18-19

The Lord is trustworthy in all he promises and faithful in all
he does. The Lord upholds all those who fall and lifts up all
who are bowed down.
Psalm 145:13-14

We all have different stories to tell, but unless you've lived under a rock your whole life, the one thing we have in common is that we have all been hurt deeply by the actions of ourselves or others at some point in our lives.

We have all made mistakes. We have all had circumstances thrust upon us that we would not necessarily have chosen for ourselves. We have all endured pain at the hands of someone else, and all of us have possibly asked at one time or another, *Is this all there is?*

The answer to that last question is a resounding *no!* Your past is *absolutely not* all there is!

God did not send His Son to die for us so that we would continue to wallow in the shame of our past and be miserable. Jesus came to give us life so we could live it to the full. However, we must never underestimate that this is a spiritual battle.

> *The thief comes only to steal and kill and destroy; I have come*
> *that they may have life and have it to the full.*
>
> *John 10:10*

We have an enemy who wants to deprive us of everything good in our lives. One of the easiest ways for him to do this is to keep us in bondage to our past, because while we are stuck there, we cannot find healing or make a positive difference in our own lives or the lives of those around us. To fully become who we were created to be, we must find freedom from the guilt and shame of our past.

It is important to be aware that whenever you begin journeying toward spiritual healing you will come under attack. The devil doesn't want you to be whole and free, and he doesn't want you to help others become whole and free either. He will do everything he can to stop you from becoming the person God intended you to be. But stand firm. As the saying goes, 'be alert but not alarmed'. In other words, be aware but don't be anxious. We have a Saviour who loves us more than anything. Jesus bore all our sins and mistakes on the cross. They are not ours to carry any longer. It is time to let them go.

Look at these two verses:

The eternal God is your refuge, and underneath are the
everlasting arms. He will drive out your enemies before
you, saying "Destroy them!"

Deuteronomy 33:27

When I said, "My foot is slipping," your unfailing
love, Lord, supported me.

Psalm 94:18

"Underneath are the everlasting arms." What a beautiful picture. His arms will never fail. He is always there, holding us up. And whenever we fall or start to slip, He will support us with His love. We can embark on this journey confident that we are not alone.

Are you ready?!

I am excited for you, and I believe God is excited for you. I believe the angels in Heaven are cheering you on to victory. And that victory has already been won for you; all you need to do now is take it. Grab it with both hands and run with it! You are beautiful, you have a purpose, and God has amazing plans for your life.

All the days ordained for me were written in your book before
one of them came to be.

Psalm 139:16

"For I know the plans I have for you," declares the Lord, "plans
to prosper you and not to harm you, plans to give you a hope
and a future."

Jeremiah 29:11

When babies learn to walk, they totter and fall but their parents are ever present, hovering close by to pick them up. Eventually they get to a point where they can get up by themselves, and although their parents are still close by, they learn to do it on their own. So, it is with us. Although our Heavenly Father is always there for us, we must eventually take responsibility for our own actions. God's grace is sufficient to cover our sins and mistakes, but it shouldn't be used as an excuse to keep making the same mistakes! Just as a child needs solid food to grow into maturity, we need to receive spiritual nourishment from the Word of God.

Hebrews 5:13-14 says:

> *For someone who lives on milk is still an infant and doesn't know how to do what is right. Solid food is for those who are mature, who through training have the skill to recognise the difference between right and wrong. (NLT)*

God has been with you throughout your life, carrying you in all your trials and difficulties, and He has brought you to this place. We cannot and must not stay trapped in the past. It is time to listen and do what He says, stand on your own two feet, and step boldly and confidently into the future that was yours before you were even born. How amazing is that? You had a plan and a purpose before you were born! Yes . . . *you!*

Think about that for a minute. There are no accidents in God's Kingdom!

Activation Questions

1. *What experiences in your life do you need supernatural healing for?*

2. *What is holding you back from receiving this healing?*

3. *What would it look like for you in the days, months or years ahead if you were fully healed?*

2

Dealing with Shame

Of all the feelings that keep us bound to our past, shame is the one that I believe holds us back the most.

Shame is what keeps us from dealing with our past.
Shame is what keeps us from voicing how we really feel.
Shame is what keeps us from allowing others to get close to us.
*Shame is what keeps us from **liking** ourselves.*

The good news is, we don't have to carry shame over our past. Jesus already carried it for us!

Therefore, since we are surrounded by such a great cloud of witnesses, let us throw off everything that hinders and the sin that so easily entangles. And let us run with perseverance the race marked out for us, fixing our eyes on Jesus, the pioneer and perfecter of faith. For the joy set before him he endured the cross, scorning its shame, and sat down at the right hand of the throne of God. Consider him who endured such opposition from sinners, so that you will not grow weary and lose heart.

Hebrews 12:1-3

When Jesus hung on the cross, He carried our mistakes, our regrets, our sin . . . and our shame. When He said, "It is finished," He was declaring our past done and dusted, paid in full.

Shame is like a disease of the soul. It eats away at us, becoming almost a 'normal' part of our existence until we believe we don't deserve to feel anything else. This is a lie of the enemy. It causes us to put on a mask that says, "I'm okay," when in reality, we are crying out for someone to help us, to share our burden, and to love us in the way we so desperately crave. Often, that leads us to look for love in all the wrong places. We enter unhealthy relationships and indulge in unhealthy lifestyle choices because we believe that we don't deserve anything better. We spend way too much time trying to 'numb the pain'.

Thankfully, there is someone who loves us unconditionally—Jesus Christ. Because of our humanness, we will inevitably feel let down or disappointed by people in our lives. We even fall short of our own expectations! But . . . there is no shame in Jesus. We can call on Him, we can give our burdens to Him, and we can trust Him.

> *See, I lay a stone in Zion, a chosen and precious cornerstone,*
> *and the one who trusts in him will never be put to shame.*
>
> *1 Peter 2:6*

In Christ we have forgiveness. We don't have to suffer for our past mistakes or hurts. We no longer have to feel like 'this is all I deserve', because that is just not true.

It is time to let go of the shame. It is time to start living the life that is yours to live—the life that God planned for you while you were still in your mother's womb. It's time to break free from negative and destructive thought patterns and begin to see yourself the way God sees you—as someone of great value and worth. Someone who is not ashamed.

Activation Questions

1. *Is shame holding you back in your life and relationships? List the things that make you feel ashamed.*

2. *When you have finished your list, lay it down on the floor (or if you are in a church setting, at the altar or underneath the cross). Then, symbolically walk away, leaving your shame behind. You may prefer to shred or burn your list instead (whatever gesture signifies to you that there is no shame left for you to carry).*

3

Freedom from Guilt

Guilt is a hard taskmaster. Sometimes, we carry guilt because of something we have done. Some people feel guilt even when they have done nothing wrong. But other times, we can be left feeling guilty about things that someone else has done to us. Why do you think this is?

I believe that we often feel unjustified or misplaced guilt because it is part of our human nature. Just think about how it feels when you get pulled over for a random breath test. I don't know about you, but I feel guilty even when I know I haven't had anything to drink! I have no reason to feel guilty, yet I still do.

But why do we feel guilty for things done to us? The reality is that when we experience abuse or trauma, we can tend to blame ourselves, leaving us with a sense of guilt over things we have no right to feel guilty about. Perhaps we believe we could have or should have done something to prevent the situation. But this is simply not true.

Therefore, there is now no condemnation for those who are in Christ Jesus, because through Christ Jesus the law of the Spirit who gives life set you free from the law of sin and death.
Romans 8:1-2

Guilt and condemnation are the tools of the devil. If we succumb to these feelings, we are giving him control over our minds and lives. We have no right to feel guilty for what someone else has done, or, for that matter, what we ourselves have done in the past. Indeed, if we have confessed our sin and received forgiveness through Jesus Christ, we can rest assured that we no longer bear any guilt.

Therefore, if anyone is in Christ, the new creation has come:
The old has gone, the new is here!

2 Corinthians 5:17

Satan wants to keep us bound to the guilt and shame of our past. It is his scheme to hold us in bondage so that we cannot move forward. However, when Jesus died on the cross, He claimed victory over the devil and paid the price for *all* our sins. Whenever we feel condemnation, we can be sure it is not of God, so we must rebuke it. The Holy Spirit convicts, but He never condemns. If we are in Christ and He is in us through the Holy Spirit, we have everything we need to stand against the ploys of the devil.

Let the beloved of the Lord rest secure in him, for he
shields him all day long and the one the Lord loves rests
between his shoulders.

Deuteronomy 33:12

This scripture is a beautiful illustration of how much God loves us. We can rest secure in Him. We don't have to do it on our own, and when we get weary from trying, we have somewhere to go.

Cast all your anxiety on him because he cares for you. Be
alert and of sober mind. Your enemy the devil prowls around
like a roaring lion looking for someone to devour. **Resist him,**
standing firm in the faith.

1 Peter 5:7-9 (emphasis mine)

Activation Questions

1.   *What does guilt feel like for you?*

2.   *What situations in your life do you feel guilty about?*

3.   *What can you do to overcome these feelings of guilt?*

4.   *You might like to say these declarations daily:*

  I, (insert your name), am a child of God.
  God loves me and sent His Son to die for me.
  I am valuable, worthy, and beautiful.
  I have nothing to feel ashamed of or guilty for!
  I will resist the devil when he tries to condemn me!

4

Dealing with Anger

Anger is a normal human reaction and emotion. We all get angry, but we need to be very careful how we express our anger. There is a fine line between being angry and being destructive in our anger. There is also a fine line between expressing our anger and holding on to it.

When we get angry, we tend to say and do things in the heat of the moment without thinking of the consequences our words and actions will have. Once a word is spoken in anger, it can never be taken back. Like a handful of dust thrown into the wind, it is impossible to retrieve. It can be months or even years before the wounds caused by a hurtful word heal. And sadly, sometimes those wounds never heal.

In your anger do not sin. Do not let the sun go down while you are still angry, and do not give the devil a foothold.
Ephesians 4:26-27

Some people stay angry and hold resentment for so long that they forget what it was that made them angry in the first place. This is why it is so important to think before we speak. In some situations, that can be easier said than done.

A gentle answer turns away wrath, but a harsh word stirs up anger. The tongue of the wise adorns knowledge, but the mouth of the fool gushes folly.
Proverbs 15:1-2

When we stay angry, we allow the devil too much space in our minds. He will say things to us like, "You will never get over this," or "You are justified to stay angry because they deserve it." We need to recognise these words for the lies they are. In their place, we should learn to recognise and listen to the voice of the Holy Spirit. His voice is the one that tells you to forgive, to let it go, and to move on.

The Psalms give us some beautiful insights into the character of God:

Sing the praises of the Lord, you his faithful people; praise his holy name. For his anger lasts only a moment, but his favour lasts a lifetime; weeping may stay for the night, but rejoicing comes in the morning.

Psalm 30:4-5

But you, Lord, are a compassionate and gracious God, slow to anger, abounding in love and faithfulness.

Psalm 86:15

There will inevitably be times in our lives when people will do and say things that cause us to become angry. Often the other person doesn't even know you are angry at them and even if they did, they might not care, so don't waste your time and energy on something that is never going to be productive in your life. Life is not always fair. Sometimes being quiet is better than being 'right'.

It is up to us how we deal with the injustices we face. We can hate, or we can forgive. We can wallow, or we can rise above it. We can stay angry and let it eat away at us, or we can let it go and move on. As we make those choices, we become more like Christ.

Finally, brothers and sisters, whatever is true, whatever is noble, whatever is right, whatever is pure, whatever is lovely, whatever is admirable—if anything is excellent or praiseworthy—think about such things. Whatever you have learned or received or heard from me or seen in me . . .

put it into practice, *and the God of peace will be with you.*
Philippians 4:8-9 (emphasis mine)

Practice thinking about what is good in your life, and you will find it is increasingly hard to stay angry and resentful. As you learn to focus on the positives, the negatives will eventually claim less and less of your mind. Living free of guilt really is possible!

Activation Questions

1. *What are some of the things that you say or do when you're angry that are not normal reactions?*

2. *What past events are you still angry about that you need to deal with?*

3. *Is there anyone you need to forgive, or feelings you need to confess, in order to let go of your anger?*

5

Learning to Forgive

I have intentionally placed the topic of forgiveness in the middle of this journey to healing. It is the turning point, the place where we finally let go of our baggage and begin to move forward into growth and wholeness.

Forgiveness needs to be directed two ways: toward others and toward ourselves.

We are often encouraged to 'forgive and forget', but it is important to remember that there is a difference between *forgetting* and *choosing not to remember*. Some things are very difficult to get over but when we truly forgive, we are not forgetting, we are choosing not to remember. We are choosing not to let past hurts or wrongs have a prominent place in our conscious memory. This is what God does for us:

> *I will forgive their wickedness and will remember*
> *their sins no more.*
>
> *Jeremiah 31:34*

I am in no way minimising the wounds some of us carry. Everyone carries their pain differently. Just because you might carry your pain differently to me does not make it any less painful, and our pain should be validated. However, it is my personal belief that the hurts that have been inflicted on us need to be put in their proper perspective—they are part of what has shaped us into who we are today but not something that should be allowed to control our future. I know from experience that it is better to walk *through* our pain than to 'set up camp' there.

Then Peter came to Jesus and asked, "Lord, how many times
shall I forgive my brother or sister who sins against me? Up to
seven times?" Jesus answered. "I tell you, not seven times, but
seventy-seven times."

Matthew 18:21-22

Bear with each other and forgive one another if any of you has
a grievance against someone. Forgive as the Lord forgave you.

Colossians 3:13

God forgave all our sins and mistakes when Jesus died on the cross
on our behalf. He bore the punishment we deserved, so is it ever right
to deny people who have hurt us that same grace? I don't think so.
Sometimes this is really hard, and the reality is that it is only by the
grace of God that we can forgive. It is not something that we can do by
ourselves, especially if the pain is too deep or we feel somehow justified
in holding a grudge because what happened to us wasn't our fault.

For if you forgive other people when they sin against you, your
heavenly Father will also forgive you. But if you do not forgive
others their sins, your Father will not forgive your sins.

Matthew 6:14-15

This verse reminds us that forgiveness is not a choice we get to make; it
is a command we must obey. In other words, unforgiveness is a sin. But
the beauty is that forgiveness does more for us than for the person we
are forgiving. When we forgive, we are setting ourselves free from the
bondage of everything we carry because of what we have experienced.
We allow ourselves to move forward and step out of the darkness that
has enveloped us for too long.

If the person who hurt us is truly remorseful, it can set them free as
well to know that they have been forgiven. On the other hand, if they
are not remorseful or even aware of your feelings, this is not your

burden to carry. They will have to give their own account for their actions, as will each of us.

In my experience, it was always easier to forgive others than it was to forgive myself. Forgiving ourselves is the biggest hurdle in the healing journey. Forgiving yourself means that you have finally become comfortable with who you are, including your past, and it is only when you have forgiven yourself that you will be able to move forward into the destiny that God has planned for you.

Sometimes, however, it is scary to forgive because it means letting go. Like children with our favourite security blanket, we hang on to certain things because it makes us feel in control—it defines who we are. But at some point, we must let go of the past in order to embrace the future. Remember, forgiveness does not mean that you are condoning what other people have done. It just means that with God's help you are willing to let it go.

Activation Questions

1. *One definition of the word forgive is: 'to cease to blame or feel resentment against'. How does it make you feel to read that, to know that if you forgive you must stop blaming and feeling resentment for what has happened to you?*

2. *What steps do you need to take to forgive the people who have hurt you?*

3. *What do you need to do to forgive yourself?*

4. *What would it mean to you to finally forgive yourself and others and be able to walk in freedom?*

6

Discovering Self-Worth

Our self-worth is intrinsically linked to what others think of us. The opinions of others, a thoughtless word, or a careless action can have an enormous impact on how we see and feel about ourselves. Instead, we should be seeking our self-worth in the One who created us. He does not make mistakes!

> *God created mankind in his own image, in the image of God he created them; male and female he created them.*
>
> *Genesis 1:27*

If we are created in the image of God, how can we be worthless? It is so easy to fall into the trap of believing the devil's lies. Whenever we make a mistake, the message we get from him is always, "See, you stuffed up again; you really are worthless."

God, on the other hand, delights in us!

> *He reached down from on high and took hold of me; he drew me out of deep waters. He rescued me from my powerful enemy, from my foes who were too strong for me. They confronted me in the day of my disaster, but the Lord was my support. He brought me out into a spacious place; he rescued me because he delighted in me.*
>
> *Psalm 18:16-19*

God delights in you! He created you for a purpose! I love those words, "He rescued me because He delighted in me." Sometimes God removes us from situations or people that are toxic to us, not to punish us, but to rescue us. I think that's amazing.

The truth is, it doesn't matter how many times we blow it, God's opinion of us never changes. And while He does use our experiences to teach or correct us, this is because He loves us and only wants the best for us.

Do not gloat over me, my enemy! Though I have fallen, I will
rise. Though I sit in darkness, the Lord will be my light.

Micah 7:8

We can take heart knowing that the Lord will be our light when everything is falling down around us, when we are being challenged and confronted to the very core of our being about who we are, and when we are being bombarded by the devil's lies. At these times we should remember that even though we might fall, God will always be there to help us up. We need to take our eyes off our circumstances and fix them on Him—the One who thought you were worth so much that He sent His Son to die for you.

Sing, Daughter Zion; shout aloud, Israel! Be glad and rejoice
with all your heart, Daughter Jerusalem! The Lord has taken
away your punishment, he has turned back your enemy.
The Lord, the King of Israel, is with you; never again will you
fear any harm. On that day they will say to Jerusalem, "Do not
fear, Zion; do not let your hands hang limp. The Lord your God
is with you, the Mighty Warrior who saves. He will take great
delight in you; in his love he will no longer rebuke you but will
rejoice over you with singing."

Zephaniah 3:14-17

"Do not let your hands hang limp." As someone who loves lifting my hands in worship, I love this expression. When you feel worthless or discouraged about who you are and where you're at, start praising God! You cannot continue to feel bad about yourself when you are praising the One who made you. Push past the negative feelings and focus on the positives in your life. They may be small and hard to find at first but the more you practice, the easier it will get.

The devil wants you to stay captive to your negative emotions and feelings. He will quite often use the people closest to us to try to bring us down. He knows that the hurtful words of a loved one or friend can do enormous damage. He doesn't want you to become all you were created to be. He feels threatened when you move forward. But God has a specific plan for your life. It's time to start believing it!

Activation Questions

1. *Read Psalm 139:1-18. Write down and memorise at least three verses from this passage that tell you how precious you are to God. Meditate on the verses you have chosen and speak them out aloud at least once a day. Personalise it by adding your own name.*

2. *Read Psalm 18:16-19. How does it feel to know that God delights in you?*

3. *Fill in the following blank: "When I feel myself getting discouraged and feeling unworthy I will _____."*

7

Choosing Confidence

We need to have confidence in ourselves to stand up for what is right, for what we believe in. Too much confidence however gives us an appearance of being arrogant, while not enough confidence will make us seem timid and meek. Confidence in its correct measure, is a good thing. So, how do we find the right balance?

> *But the fruit of the Spirit is love, joy, peace, patience, kindness, goodness, faithfulness, gentleness, and self-control. Against such things there is no law.*
>
> *Galatians 5:22-23*

Living by these words will give us the right balance. Each of these words gives us the qualities we need to have confidence not just in who we are, but more importantly, in who God is. Ultimately, our confidence needs to lie in God.

If you are facing a difficult situation, or you are feeling overwhelmed or discouraged—give it to God. You can give it all to Him in prayer.

> *Give all your worries and cares to God, for he cares about you.*
>
> *1 Peter 5:7 NLT*

When you are confident about who you are in Christ, the challenges you are facing won't seem so big, the despair you are feeling won't seem so dark.

> *Don't let your hearts be troubled. Trust in God, trust also in me.*
>
> *John 14:1 NLT*

You are beautiful! You are vibrant! You were made for a purpose! You are fearfully and wonderfully made. If God has enough confidence in you to fulfil your destiny, then why fight it? Step up and become all you were created to be!

> *You, dear children, are from God and have overcome them, because the one who is in you is greater than the one who is in the world.*
>
> 1 John 4:4

> *I thank my God every time I remember you. In all my prayers for all of you I always pray with joy because of your partnership in the gospel from the first day until now,* **being confident of this***, that he who began a good work in you will carry it on to completion until the day of Christ Jesus.*
>
> Philippians 1:3-6 (emphasis mine)

> *God is not human, that he should lie, not a human being, that he should change his mind. Does he speak and then not act? Does he promise and not fulfill?*
>
> Numbers 23:19

God does not make mistakes, nor does He change His mind. If He has begun a good work in you, be confident that He will be there to help you every step of the way.

Activation Questions

1. *Read Galatians 5:22-23. Name the characteristics in this scripture that you can identify in your life. Then name the characteristics that you would like to see become more evident in your life.*

2. *Memorise Philippians 1:6, then speak it out and start believing it!*

8

Finding Your Strength

If your past is something that has often defined and shaped you, then letting go of it requires a great deal of strength and courage. Where does this strength come from?

> *And the God of all grace, who called you to his eternal glory in Christ, after you have suffered a little while, will himself restore you and make you strong, firm, and steadfast.*
>
> *1 Peter 5:10*

Our strength comes from the Lord. It is true that going through the process of letting go is very difficult. But there is more power in submitting to God's will for our life than there is in trying to do it on our own. We all face suffering in one way or another, but God will ultimately refine and restore us into the people we were meant to be.

> *Yet you, Lord, are our Father. We are the clay, you are the potter; we are all the work of your hand.*
>
> *Isaiah 64:8*

God created all of us for a purpose but somewhere along the way we have messed things up. We have tried to address issues in our own strength, thinking we were capable, and giving the illusion that we had it all together. But ultimately there comes a point where we must throw up our hands and say, "I can't do this on my own!"

I believe God loves hearing us say that. In response, He picks us up, dusts us off, and says, "It's okay, I'm with you. You don't have to do it on your own."

You may already have come to that point. You've had enough of the pain and suffering, of just going through the motions, existing through life instead of living it. It's time to be restored to the beautiful, vibrant, strong person that God created and intended you to be. You *can* break the cycle! You can be the one who stands up and takes back what is rightfully yours—your destiny, and your future in Christ Jesus. Just because something has always been, doesn't mean it always will be. Seek your strength from the Lord and see where He can take you!

Do not fear, for I am with you; do not be dismayed, for I am your God. I will strengthen you and help you; I will uphold you with my righteous right hand.

Isaiah 41:10

The name of the Lord is a fortified tower; the righteous run to it and are safe.

Proverbs 18:10

It's easy to get bogged down in our feelings, but let's run to Him and find safety. The end result will always be worth it. We can be strong in the knowledge that God is always with us.

Activation Questions

1. *In the past, where have you tended to draw your strength from?*

2. *What keeps you from truly believing that God can help you and will strengthen you?*

3. *2 Corinthians 12:9 says, "My grace is sufficient for you, for my power is made perfect in weakness." Make the decision today to allow God to be your strength, to truly give it all to Him, and to allow His strength to shine through your weakness.*

9

Freedom from Fear

Fear can be crippling. It can control our thoughts and our actions. Sometimes, fear keeps us from trying new things because we are afraid we will fail. But when it comes to letting go of our past and moving on, we sometimes hesitate because we are afraid we will succeed. It can feel easier to hold on to the shame and guilt of our past than to admit that it has become a crutch for us to lean on. In Christ, however, we are a new creation.

For God has not given us a spirit of fear, but of power and of love and of a sound mind.

2 Timothy 1:7 NKJV

Therefore, if anyone is in Christ, the new creation has come: The old has gone, the new is here!

2 Corinthians 5:17

So, if God has given us a spirit of power, love, and a sound mind, and if we are indeed a new creation in Christ, then why do we find it so hard to let things go?

Perhaps we are afraid of losing control. Hanging on to the past is the safe option because in some ways, it is our security. It has been such a big part of who we are, and has defined us for so long, that to let it go would mean losing a big part of our identity. The apostle Paul grappled with this as well. He wrote:

Not that I have already obtained all this, or have already arrived at my goal, but I press on to take hold of that for which

*Christ Jesus took hold of me. Brothers and sisters, I do not
consider myself yet to have taken hold of it. But one thing I do:
Forgetting what is behind and straining toward what is ahead,
I press on toward the goal to win the prize for which God has
called me heavenward in Christ Jesus.*

Philippians 3:12-14

God has a purpose for you. Jesus died so that you could fulfil that
purpose, but you must first let go of your past. God cannot do the
things He desires to do in you and through you if you are continually
pulling back from Him, or not acknowledging His sovereignty over
your life and allowing Him to do what only He can do.

*Jesus replied, "No one who puts his hand to the plow and looks
back is fit for service in the kingdom of God."*

Luke 9:62

We must look beyond our past mistakes and hurts. If we keep looking
back, we will continue to stumble and fall because we are not looking
where we are going. You can't drive a car by looking in the rearview
mirror all the time. You will end up crashing if you don't look forward!
In the same way, we need to fix our eyes on Jesus and His love, not on
things like shame and unforgiveness.

*. . . fixing our eyes on Jesus, the pioneer and perfecter of faith.
For the joy set before him he endured the cross, scorning its
shame, and sat down at the right hand of the throne of God.
Consider him who endured such opposition from sinners, so
that you will not grow weary and lose heart.*

Hebrews 12:2-3

God wants to use us for greater purposes! No one ever said it was going
to be easy—remember, when we begin to grow and change into the
people God created us to be, we will encounter opposition from the

devil, from other people, and from ourselves! Never underestimate the spiritual battle. The enemy wants to keep us bound to our past, and he will use whatever means necessary to keep us stuck there—even the people closest to us at times. Your family and friends may be confronted or even threatened by your newfound freedom and strength. This was certainly my experience. My ex-husband was very threatened by the strength and confidence I gained as I began to heal. It ultimately cost me my marriage. But as I let go of fear, I ended up gaining so much more.

When I am afraid, I put my trust in you.

Psalm 56:3

There is no fear in love. But perfect love drives out fear, because fear has to do with punishment. The one who fears is not made perfect in love.

1 John 4:18

We can sabotage ourselves by hanging on to the 'victim mentality', by refusing to accept that we can ever be anything other than what we are. You have already started journeying toward your healing. The rest is up to you. From this day forward you need to make the choice to allow God to help you let go and move on—or to stay bound to your past and let the enemy win. It's totally up to you. I encourage you to 'let go and let God'!

To him who is able to keep you from stumbling and to present you before his glorious presence without fault and with great joy—to the only God our Saviour be glory, majesty, power and authority, through Jesus Christ our Lord, before all ages, now and forevermore! Amen.

Jude 1:24-25

Activation Questions

1. *Look back over your answers to the questions right at the start of this journey. Have you begun to move toward where you wanted to be? Why or why not?*

2. *What further steps could you take to achieve complete healing of your past?*

10

Learning to Overcome

Congratulations! You have already taken the first step by bravely and honestly working through these issues. Now you have the opportunity to move forward—to see the road before you and to know that you can walk it with fresh hope.

The rest is up to you. You have the choice to take what you have learned and apply it to your life—or not. This is your opportunity to overcome, in other words, to conquer, or get the upper hand, in whatever conflict or struggle you have been facing.

> *Do not be overcome by evil but overcome evil with good.*
>
> *Romans 12:21*

> *I am coming soon. Hold on to what you have, so that no one will take your crown. The one who is victorious I will make a pillar in the temple of my God. Never again will they leave it. I will write on them the name of my God and the name of the city of my God, the new Jerusalem, which is coming down out of heaven from my God; and I will also write on them my new name.*
>
> *Revelation 3:11-12*

God has a new name for us. Unlike the names we have been known by in our past (unworthy, failure, unlovely, oppressed, ashamed, guilty), we will be called strong, beautiful, worthy, successful, lovable, unashamed, forgiven!

We have the victory! Jesus claimed it for us when He died on the cross. But we cannot be passive onlookers. We must take what we have been given and run with it. Let's defy the enemy and live the life that God has given us!

The thief comes only to steal and kill and destroy; I have come that they may have life and have it to the full.

John 10:10

You cannot live life to the full if you are continually living in your past. The devil wants to keep you bound to the hurt and shame you have experienced, but enough is enough! With God at your side, you can move on.

Remember, you are a beautiful child of God and nothing God does is weak. When you put your trust and faith in Him and His power to change your story, you will find strength to overcome your past and move forward into your future.

In all these things we are more than conquerors through him who loved us.

Romans 8:37

To *overcome* is to defeat, conquer, win. Start speaking these words over your life: I can **overcome** negative thought patterns; I can **defeat** the enemy and his lies; I am a **conqueror**; and **I will win!**

But thanks be to God! He gives us the victory through our Lord Jesus Christ. Therefore, my dear brothers and sisters, stand firm. Let nothing move you. Always give yourselves fully to the work of the Lord, because you know that your labour in the Lord is not in vain.

1 Corinthians 15:57-58

Stand firm! Accept yourself as God sees you. God's work is never in vain, so rest assured that the work He is doing in you is good. His plans for you are incredible. You have been forgiven. You are healing. And you were made for a purpose.

It's time to rise above your past and step into a future that is ready and waiting for you to take hold of it. Yes, it is a struggle. And yes, sometimes it will be hard. But I firmly believe that if we keep our focus on God and His Word, we can overcome all things, even our past.

> *"For I know the plans I have for you," declares the Lord,*
> *"plans to prosper you and not to harm you, plans to give*
> *you a hope and a future."*
>
> *Jeremiah 29:11*

The victory is yours . . . now go ahead and take it!

Acknowledgements

Any book needs a lot of people to make it work, and this one is no exception. I want to thank everyone who has encouraged me to put my story into print. I am so blessed to be surrounded by such a wonderful group of people but there are a few who need a special mention here. So, in no particular order, acknowledgement goes to:

James. Thank you for letting me share our story within my story. I still pinch myself when I think about how God brought us together and how He knew we would be so perfect for each other, despite our obvious differences! We have overcome so much as we have built our dream together. You are such a man of integrity. I will always be proud to be your wife and I love being your brown-eyed girl. Team Southwell. Better Together.

Emmie. We met as work colleagues all those years ago, now I am blessed to call you one of my closest friends. Thank you for your friendship, the coffees, your wisdom and insight and the many hours you put in to proofread my original ramblings to get them to a point where they made sense.

Colleen. You helped me survive the valley that was 2010. Thank you for being my 'bodyguard', one of my dearest friends, and the reason I kept going to church when I had dozens of reasons to walk away.

The other half of Team Wilwell. You guys are definitely our 'Aaron and Hur'. You inspire us, you challenge us, you make us laugh. I am so very grateful to have you in our lives.

Shania. You broke the chains before the chains broke you. In one beautifully God-ordained moment, our hearts were eternally connected

...and although our stories are different, you are the personification of who this book is written for. Keep being who He created you to be. Beautiful. Brave. Uncompromising.

Jim and Kellie. There are no words to adequately describe how we feel about you guys. This story would never have reached its current conclusion if not for you. I know God is not finished with any of us and our hilarious stories and friendship will continue to grow, no matter where life takes us. Thank you for being our Proverbs 27:17 friends—"As iron sharpens iron, so a friend sharpens a friend."

Joel and Grace. What a ride this has been. We were all together for just a season but what a season it turned out to be! A brief moment in time that will, no doubt, have eternal consequences. 'For such a time as this'. God is so good.

Ps Gary and Raylene. Thank you for welcoming us, loving us, and allowing me to share my story. We are so grateful that God led us to 'The Vine'!

Ps Steve and Deb. We love you, we honour you and we're blessed to call you friends.

Anya McKee and the team at Torn Curtain Publishing. Thank you for your wisdom, patience and grace in bringing this book to fruition. But most of all, thank you for believing in me and for the way you so beautifully helped me find my voice and bring Michael's story to life.

Michael, and all the other babies like you. You mattered.

And, above all, Jesus. The One who was always there. The One who never left. The One who took my mess and turned it into a powerful message. I am so humbled, and I am so grateful.

May these words of my mouth and this meditation of my heart be pleasing in your sight, LORD, my rock and my redeemer.

A Note from the Author

The book you have just read has been a fifteen-year labour of love. I first started writing it in 2008 when I felt the prompting to share my story after the women's conference I talked about at the beginning. It has been very therapeutic to write as it has gone from an initial angry word dump to the fully and professionally edited version you hold in your hands, with many different iterations in between!

As He has done so many times before, God has taken me on another detour since finishing this manuscript.

Finishing our house, and me coming off staff at the church we were at has coincided with a move—to a new state, a new church, and a new home. It has been the ending of the old season where it was more than time to say goodbye, and the beginning of the new season, where we have already been embraced with warm hellos.

I firmly believe God positioned me exactly where He needed me to be for the events in this book to come to their conclusion, while already knowing where He would lead me next. I am grateful for the experience, and I have come out the other side, stronger, wiser, and ready to take on the next chapter . . . whatever that looks like!

If any of my story has resonated with you, please take a moment to reach out. I would love to hear about it! You can email me at:

enjoyingthedetour@gmail.com

About the Author

Vikki Southwell is a born and bred Australian author. She loves 'getting away from it all' by going camping or bushwalking. Apart from writing, her creative passion is photography, and she is happiest snapping shots of the beautiful Australian landscape. After growing up in the 'big smoke' she now lives on acreage in rural New South Wales with her husband James, a crazy Golden Retriever named Holly, and a cantankerous but endearing seventeen-year-old cat named Coco, with plenty of space for when their blended family of adult children and grandchildren come to visit!

Vikki is passionate about seeing people get set free from their past and draws on her life experiences and faith in God to point others toward finding their own healing and freedom.

For speaking engagements or other enquiries, please get in touch with Vikki at:

Email: enjoyingthedetour@gmail.com

Facebook: @Enjoying the detour

Instagram: @enjoying_thedetour

Made in the USA
Las Vegas, NV
13 January 2024

84325937R00083